COMPUTER SCIENCE, TECHNOLOGY AND APPLICATIONS

PEER-TO-PEER STORAGE: SECURITY AND PROTOCOLS

COMPUTER SCIENCE, TECHNOLOGY AND APPLICATIONS

Mobile Computing Research and Applications
Kevin Y. Chen and H.K. Lee (Editors)
2009. ISBN 978-1-60741-101-7

Large Scale Computations, Embedded Systems and Computer Security
Fedor Komarov and Maksim Bestuzhev (Editors)
2009. ISBN: 978-1-60741-307-3

Problem Solving with Delphi - CD included
Stephen John Sugden
2009. ISBN 978-1-60741-249-6

Performance Modelling Techniques for Parallel Supercomputing Applications
A. Grove and P.D. Coddington
2010. ISBN: 9781-60692-269-9

Relational Databases and Open Source Software Developments
Jennifer R. Taylor (Editor)
2010. ISBN: 978-1-61668-436-5
2010. ISBN: 978-1-61668-468-6
(E-book)

Data Mining and Management
Lawrence I. Spendler (Editor)
2010. ISBN: 978-1-60741-289-2

Biometrics: Methods, Applications and Analyses
Harvey Schuster and Wilfred Metzger (Editors)
2010. ISBN: 978-1-60876-412-9

Computer Animation
Jaron S. Wright and Lloyd M. Hughes (Editors)
2010. ISBN: 978-1-60741-559-6

Java Software and Embedded Systems
Mattis Hayes and Isaiah Johansen (Editors)
2010. ISBN: 978-1-60741-661-6

Computer Games: Learning Objectives, Cognitive Performance and Effects on Development
Agustin Soria and Julián Maldonado (Editors)
2010. ISBN: 978-1-60876-658-1

Computer Communication for Metropolitan and Wide Area Networks
Matthew N. O. Sadiku and Sarhan M. Musa
2010. ISBN: 978-1-61668-024-4

Peer-to-Peer Networks and Internet Policies
Diego Vegros and Jaime Sáenz (Editors)
2010. ISBN: 978-1-60876-287-3

Computational Mechanics Research Trends
Hans P. Berger (Editor)
2010. ISBN: 978-1-60876-057-2

Design and Performance of Biometric System
John T. Elsworth (Editor)
2010. ISBN: 978-1-60692-978-0
2010. ISBN: 978-1-61668-524-9
(E-book)

Intuition and Computer Programming (WT)
Michael Weigend
2010. ISBN: 978-1-61668-330-6
2010. ISBN: 978-1-61668-813-4
(E-book)

Biometrics, Privacy, Progress and Government
Rachel B. Jefferson (Editor)
2010. ISBN: 978-1-60741-098-0

Agent-Based Computing
Duarte Bouça and Amaro Gafagnão (Editors)
2010. ISBN: 978-1-60876-684-0

Wireless Sensor Networks
Liam I. Farrugia (Editor)
2010. ISBN: 978-1-61728-125-9
2010. ISBN: 978-1-61728-328-4
(E-book)

3D Imaging: Theory, Technology and Applications
Emerson H. Duke and Stephen R. Aguirre (Editors)
2010. ISBN: 978-1-60876-885-1

Peer-to-Peer Storage: Security and Protocols
Nouha Oualha and Yves Roudier
2010. ISBN: 978-1-61668-199-9
2010. ISBN: 978-1-61668-462-4
(E-book)

Persuasion On-Line and Communicability: The Destruction of Credibility in the Virtual Community and Cognitive Models
Francisco V. Cipolla-Ficarra
2010. ISBN: 978-1-61668-268-2
2010. ISBN: 978-1-61668-701-4
(E-book)

Semantic Web: Standards, Tools and Ontologies
Kimberly A. Haffner (Editor)
2010. ISBN: 978-1-61668-471-6
2010. ISBN: 978-1-61668-540-9
(E-book)

**Logic of Analog
and Digital Machines**
Paolo Rocchi
2010. ISBN: 978-1-61668-481-5
2010. ISBN: 978-1-61668-815-8
(E-book)

**Practice and Research Notes in
Relational Database Applications**
Haitao Yang
2010. ISBN: 978-1-61668-850-9
2010. ISBN: 978-1-61728-460-1
(E-book)

COMPUTER SCIENCE, TECHNOLOGY AND APPLICATIONS

PEER-TO-PEER STORAGE: SECURITY AND PROTOCOLS

NOUHA OUALHA AND YVES ROUDIER

Nova Science Publishers, Inc.
New York

Copyright © 2010 by Nova Science Publishers, Inc.

All rights reserved. No part of this book may be reproduced, stored in a retrieval system or transmitted in any form or by any means: electronic, electrostatic, magnetic, tape, mechanical photocopying, recording or otherwise without the written permission of the Publisher.

For permission to use material from this book please contact us:
Telephone 631-231-7269; Fax 631-231-8175
Web Site: http://www.novapublishers.com

NOTICE TO THE READER

The Publisher has taken reasonable care in the preparation of this book, but makes no expressed or implied warranty of any kind and assumes no responsibility for any errors or omissions. No liability is assumed for incidental or consequential damages in connection with or arising out of information contained in this book. The Publisher shall not be liable for any special, consequential, or exemplary damages resulting, in whole or in part, from the readers' use of, or reliance upon, this material. Any parts of this book based on government reports are so indicated and copyright is claimed for those parts to the extent applicable to compilations of such works.

Independent verification should be sought for any data, advice or recommendations contained in this book. In addition, no responsibility is assumed by the publisher for any injury and/or damage to persons or property arising from any methods, products, instructions, ideas or otherwise contained in this publication.

This publication is designed to provide accurate and authoritative information with regard to the subject matter covered herein. It is sold with the clear understanding that the Publisher is not engaged in rendering legal or any other professional services. If legal or any other expert assistance is required, the services of a competent person should be sought. FROM A DECLARATION OF PARTICIPANTS JOINTLY ADOPTED BY A COMMITTEE OF THE AMERICAN BAR ASSOCIATION AND A COMMITTEE OF PUBLISHERS.

LIBRARY OF CONGRESS CATALOGING-IN-PUBLICATION DATA

Available upon request.
ISBN : 978-1-61668-199-9

Published by Nova Science Publishers, Inc. † New York

CONTENTS

Preface		ix
Chapter I	Introduction	1
Chapter II	Trust Establishment	7
Chapter III	Remote Data Possession Verification	13
Chapter IV	Cooperation Incentives	29
Chapter V	Validation Based On Game Theory	37
Chapter VI	Conclusion	49
References		51
Index		59

PREFACE

Peer-to-peer (P2P) has proven as a most successful way to produce large scale, reliable, and cost-effective applications, as illustrated for file sharing or VoIP. P2P storage is an emerging field of application which allows peers to collectively leverage their resources towards ensuring the reliability and availability of user data. Providing assurances in both domains requires not only ensuring the confidentiality and privacy of the data storage process, but also thwarting peer misbehavior through the introduction of proper security and cooperation enforcement mechanisms. Misbehavior may consist in data destruction or corruption by malicious or free-riding peers. Additionally, a new form of man-in-the-middle attack may make it possible for a malicious peer to pretend to be storing data without using any local disk space. New forms of collusion also may occur whereby replica holders would collude to store a single replica of some data, thereby defeating the requirement of data redundancy. Finally, Sybil attackers may create a large number of identities and use them to gain a disproportionate personal advantage.The continuous observation of peer behavior and monitoring of the storage process is an important requirement to secure a storage system. Observing peer misbehavior requires appropriate primitives like proofs of data possession, a form of proof of knowledge whereby the holder interactively tries to convince the verifier that it possesses the very data without actually retrieving them or copying them at verifier's memory. We present a survey of such techniques and discuss their suitability for assessing remote data storage.

Cooperation is key to deploying P2P storage solutions, yet peers in such applications are confronted to an inherent social dilemma: should they contribute to the collective welfare or misbehave for their individual welfare?

We review several incentive mechanisms that have been proposed to stimulate cooperation towards achieving a resilient storage.

The effectiveness of such incentive mechanisms must be validated for a large-scale system. We describe how this can be assessed with game theoretical techniques. In this approach, cooperation incentive mechanisms are proven to be effective if it is demonstrated that any rational peer will always choose to follow mechanism directives whenever it interacts with another peer. We finally illustrate the validation of cooperation incentives with one-stage and repeated cooperative and non cooperative games and evolutionary games.

Chapter I - Self-organization has first emerged, in the late 90's, as specialized systems and protocols to support peer-to-peer (P2P) file sharing. It became very popular thanks to services like Napster, Gnutella, KaZaA and Morpheus, and particularly to the legal controversy regarding their copyrighted contents. Since then, the popularity of P2P systems has continued to grow such that self-organization is now regarded as a general-purpose and practical approach that can be applied to designing applications for resource sharing. Resources in this context may include the exchange of information, processing cycles, packet forwarding and routing, as well as cache and disk storage. In this sense, self-organization, as revealed in P2P, is being increasingly used in several application domains ranging from P2P telephony or audio/video streaming to ad hoc networks or nomadic computing. P2P storage services have more recently been suggested as a new technique to make use of the vast and untapped storage resources available on personal computers. P2P data storage services like Wuala, AllMyData Tahoe, and UbiStorage have received some highlight. In all of these, data is outsourced from the data owner place to several heterogonous storage sites in the network, in order to increase data availability and fault-tolerance, to reduce storage maintenance costs, and to achieve a high scalability of the system.

Chapter II - In P2P systems, peers often must interact with unknown or unfamiliar peers without the help of trusted third parties or authorities to mediate the interactions. As a result, peers trying to establish trust towards other peers generally rely on cooperation as evaluated on some period of time. The rationale behind such trust is that peers have confidence if the other peers cooperate by joining their efforts and actions for a common benefit. P2P systems are inherently large scale, highly churned out, and relatively anonymous systems; volunteer cooperation is thus hardly achievable. Building trust in such systems is the key step towards the adoption of this kind of systems and relies on providing some assurance on the effective cooperative behavior of peers.

Trust between peers can be achieved in two essential ways that depend on the type and extent of trust relationships among peers and that reflect the models and trends in P2P. Static trust based schemes rely on stable and preexisting relationships between peers, while dynamic trust is relying on a realtime assessment of peer behavior.

Other taxonomies have been proposed. classifies cooperation enforcement mechanisms into trust-based patterns and trade-based patterns. Obreiter et al. distinguish between static trust, thereby referring to pre-established trust between peers, and dynamic trust, by which they refer to reputation-based trust. They analyze trade-based patterns as being based either on immediate or on deferred remuneration. Other authors describe cooperation in self-organized systems only in terms of reputation based and remuneration based approaches. Trust establishment, a further step in many protocols, easily maps to reputation but may rely on remuneration as well. In this work, we adhere to the existing classification of cooperation incentives in distinguishing between reputation-based and remuneration-based approaches.

Chapter III - Self-organizing data storage must ensure data availability on a long term basis. This objective requires developing appropriate primitives for detecting dishonest peers free riding on the self-organizing storage infrastructure. Assessing such a behavior is the objective of data possession verification protocols. In contrast with simple integrity checks, which make sense only with respect to a potentially defective yet trusted server, verifying the remote data possession aims at detecting voluntary data destructions by a remote peer. These primitives have to be efficient: in particular, verifying the presence of these data remotely should not require transferring them back in their entirety; it should neither make it necessary to store the entire data at the verifier. The latter requirement simply forbids the use of plain message integrity codes as a protection measure since it prevents the construction of time-variant challenges based on such primitives.

Chapter IV - Cooperation enforcement is a central feature of P2P systems, and even more so self-organizing systems, to compensate for the lack of a dedicated and trusted coordinator and still get some work done. However, cooperation to achieve some functionality is not necessarily an objective of peers that are not under the control of any authority and that may try to maximize the benefits they get from the P2P system. Cooperation incentive schemes have been introduced to stimulate the cooperation of such self-interested peers. They are diverse not only in terms of the applications which they protect, but also in terms of the features they implement, the type of reward and punishment used, and their operation over time. Cooperation incentives are classically classified into barter-based, reputation-based, and remuneration-based approaches.

Chapter V - Cooperation incentives prevent selfish behaviors whereby peers free-ride the storage system, that is, they store data onto other peers without contributing to the storage infrastructure. Remote data verification protocols are required to implement the auditing mechanism needed by any efficient cooperation incentive mechanism. In general, a cooperation incentive mechanism is proven to be effective if it is demonstrated that any rational peer will always choose to cooperate whenever it interacts with another cooperative peer. One-stage games or repeated games have been mostly used to validate cooperation incentives that describe individual strategies; in addition, the use of evolutionary dynamics can help describe the evolution of strategies within large populations.

Chapter VI - Peer-to-Peer (P2P) systems have emerged as an important paradigm for distributed storage in that they aim at efficiently exploiting untapped storage resources available in a wide base of peers. Data are outsourced to several heterogonous storage sites in the network, the major expected outcome being an increased data availability and reliability, while also achieving reduced storage maintenance costs, and high scalability. Addressing security issues in such P2P storage applications represents an indispensable part of the solution satisfying these requirements. Security relies on low level cryptographic primitives, remote data possession verification protocols, for observing malicious and selfish behaviors. Such an assessment of peer behavior is crucial to the more complex enforcement of cooperation, which is necessary due to the self-organized nature of P2P networks. It is also crucial to address open issues, such as how to mitigate denial of service attempts to the long-term storage as well as to the security and storage maintenance functions.

Chapter I

INTRODUCTION

Self-organization has first emerged, in the late 90's, as specialized systems and protocols to support peer-to-peer (P2P) file sharing. It became very popular thanks to services like Napster [70], Gnutella [34], KaZaA [46] and Morpheus [66], and particularly to the legal controversy regarding their copyrighted contents. Since then, the popularity of P2P systems has continued to grow such that self-organization is now regarded as a general-purpose and practical approach that can be applied to designing applications for resource sharing. Resources in this context may include the exchange of information, processing cycles, packet forwarding and routing, as well as cache and disk storage. In this sense, self-organization, as revealed in P2P, is being increasingly used in several application domains ranging from P2P telephony or audio/video streaming to ad hoc networks or nomadic computing. P2P storage services have more recently been suggested as a new technique to make use of the vast and untapped storage resources available on personal computers. P2P data storage services like Wuala [97], AllMyData Tahoe [3], and UbiStorage [93] have received some highlight. In all of these, data is outsourced from the data owner place to several heterogonous storage sites in the network, in order to increase data availability and fault-tolerance, to reduce storage maintenance costs, and to achieve a high scalability of the system.

A. A Case for P2P Storage

Innovation and advancement in information technology has spurred a tremendous growth in the amount of data available and generated. This has generated new challenges regarding scalable storage management that must be addressed by implementing storage applications in a self-organized and cooperative form. In such storage applications, peers can store their personal data in one or multiple copies (replication) at other peers. The latter, called *holders*, should store data until the owner retrieves them. Such P2P storage aims at maintaining a reliable storage without a single point of failure, although without the need for an expensive and energy-consuming storage infrastructure as offered by data centers. Peers volunteer for holding data within their own storage space on a long term basis while they expect a reciprocal behavior from other peers.

P2P storage has been presented as a solution for data backup ([49] and [55]) as well as for a new generation of distributed file systems ([81], [44], and [86]). P2P storage aims at a free and more importantly more resilient alternative to centralized storage, in particular to address the fact that storage can still be considered as a single point of failure. Additionally, P2P storage may also be attractive in wireless ad-hoc networks or delay-tolerant networks (DTNs), notably since mobility introduces a store-carry-and-forward paradigm ([96]) to deliver packets despite frequent and extended network partitions. The cooperative storage of other nodes' messages until their delivery to their destination thus might become an important feature of such networks. Context- or location-based services may also benefit from P2P storage. Desktop teleporting ([28], [90]) for instance aims at the dynamic mapping of the desktop of a user onto a specific location. Teleporting may make use of the storage offered by surrounding nodes at the new user location. Location-aware information delivery ([71], [5], [6], [57]) is another context-aware application. Each reminder message is created with a location, and when the intended recipient arrives at that location, the message is delivered. The remainder message may be stored at nodes situated nearby the location context rather than at the mobile node.

Though the self-organization introduced by P2P storage promises to produce large scale, reliable, and cost-effective applications, it exposes the stored data to new threats. In particular, P2P systems and, even more so, P2P storage systems may be subject to selfishness, a misbehavior whereby peers may discard some data they promised to store for other peers in order to optimize their resource usage. Maliciousness in the P2P context woult simply consist in peers destroying the data they store in order to reduce the quality of service of the system. Because of the high churn and dynamics of peers, checking that some data have been stored somewhere is quite more complex than checking that a route has been established with another node in multi-hop

MANETs for instance. In addition, such verifications cannot be instantaneous but have to be repeatedly performed. All these problems contribute to the difficulty of properly determining the actual availability of data stored onto unknown peers. Countermeasures that take into account the fact that users have full authority on their devices should be crafted to prevent them from cheating the system in order to maximize the benefit they can obtain out of peer cooperation.

B. Security Objectives

A P2P storage application takes advantage of the existing and spare disk space at peers allowing the latter to leverage their collective power for the *common good*. While the fundamental premise of this is voluntary storage resource sharing among individual peers, there is an inherent tension between individual rationality and collective welfare that threatens the viability of these applications. This behavior, termed *free riding*, is the result of a social dilemma that all peers confront and may lead to system collapse in *the tragedy of the commons* [29]: the dilemma for each peer is to either contribute to the common good, or to free ride (shirk).

Achieving secure and trusted P2P storage presents a particular challenge in that context due to the open, autonomous, and highly dynamic nature of P2P networks. We argue that any effort to protect the P2P storage system should ensure the following goals.

Confidentiality and Integrity of Data

Most storage applications deal with personal (or group) data that are stored somewhere in the network at peers that are not especially trusted. Data must thus be protected while transmitted to and stored at some peer. Typically, the confidentiality and the integrity of stored data are ensured using usual cryptographic means such as encryption methods and checksums.

Anonymity

Anonymity can be a requirement for some type of storage applications that aim at preventing information censorship for instance; however it may not be a targeted objective for all of them. Anonymity may refer to the data owner identity, the data holder identity, or the detail of their interaction. Anonymity permits to avoid attacks whereby the data of a given user are specifically targeted in order to destroy them from the system. Systems that seek to provide anonymity often employ infrastructures for providing anonymous connection layers, e.g., onion routing [18].

Identification

Within a distributed environment like P2P, it is possible for the same physical entity to appear under different identities, particularly in systems with highly transient populations of peers. This problem may lead to attacks called "Sybil attacks" [45], and may also threaten mechanisms such as data replication that rely on the existence of independent peers with different identities. Solutions to these attacks may rely on the deployment of a trusted third party acting as a central certification authority, yet this approach may limit anonymity. Alternatively, P2P storage may be operated by some authority controlling the network through the payment of membership fees to limit the introduction of fake identities. However, that approach reduces the decentralized nature of P2P systems and introduces a single point of failure or slows the bootstrap of the system if payment involves real money. Without a trusted third party, another option is to bootstrap the system through penalties imposed on all newcomers: an insider peer may only probabilistically cooperate with newcomers (like in the P2P file sharing application BitTorrent [58]), or peers may join the system only if an insider peer with limited invitation tickets invites them [26]. The acceptable operations for a peer may also be limited if the connection of too many ephemeral and untrustworthy identities is observed [37]. This option however seems to be detrimental to the scalability of the system and it has even been shown that this degrades the total social welfare [59]. Social networks may also partially solve the identification issue.

Access Control

Encryption is a basic mechanism to enforce access control with respect to read operations. The lack of authentication can be overcome by the distribution of the keys necessary for accessing the stored data to a subset of privileged peers. Access control lists can also be assigned to data by their original owners through the use of signed certificates. Capability-based access control can be also employed like in [67]. Delete operations have to be especially controlled because of their potentially devastating end result.

Scalability

The system should be able to scale to a large population of peers. Since most of the important functions of the system are performed by peers, the

Introduction 5

system should then be able to handle growing amounts of control messages for peer and storage resource management and an increased complexity in a graceful manner. The system may also be clustered into small groups with homogeneous storage needs which may reduce the load over peers.

Data Reliability

The common technique to achieve data reliability relies on data redundancy at several locations in the network. The data may be simply replicated at a given redundancy factor. The redundancy factor should be maintained during the entire duration of the data storage. The rejuvenation of the data may be carried out either in a periodic or event-driven fashion. For instance, in the latter approach, one or multiple new replicas should be generated whenever a certain number of replicas have been detected as destroyed or corrupted. Other redundancy schemes may be used instead of merely replicating the data into identical copies; for instance erasure coding provides the same level of data reliability with much lower storage costs.

Long-Term Data Survivability

The durability of storage in some applications like backup is very critical. The system must ensure that the data will be permanently conserved (until their retrieval by the owner). Techniques such as data replication or erasure coding improve the durability of data conservation but these techniques must be regularly adjusted to maximize the capacity of the system to tolerate failures. Generally, the employed adaptation method is based on frequent checks over the data stored to test whether the various fragments of a data are held by separate holders. Moreover, cooperation incentive techniques must be used to encourage holders to preserve the data they store as long as they can.

Data Availability

Any storage system must ensure that stored data are accessible and useable upon demand by an authorized peer. Data checks at holders allow the regular verification of this property. The intermittent connectivity of holders can be tolerated by applying a "grace period" through which the verifiers tolerate no response from the checked holder for a given number of challenges before declaring it non cooperative.

The rest of this chapter especially details how to achieve the last three objectives above: high reliability, availability, and long-term durability of data storage in the context of a large scale P2P storage system. These three objectives are often ignored in P2P file sharing applications which rather follow best effort approaches. Performing periodic cryptographic verifications makes it possible to evaluate the security status of data stored in the system and to design an adapted cooperation incentive framework for securing data storage in the long run.

Chapter II

TRUST ESTABLISHMENT

In P2P systems, peers often must interact with unknown or unfamiliar peers without the help of trusted third parties or authorities to mediate the interactions. As a result, peers trying to establish trust towards other peers generally rely on cooperation as evaluated on some period of time. The rationale behind such trust is that peers have confidence if the other peers cooperate by joining their efforts and actions for a common benefit. P2P systems are inherently large scale, highly churned out, and relatively anonymous systems; volunteer cooperation is thus hardly achievable. Building trust in such systems is the key step towards the adoption of this kind of systems and relies on providing some assurance on the effective cooperative behavior of peers.

Trust between peers can be achieved in two essential ways that depend on the type and extent of trust relationships among peers and that reflect the models and trends in P2P systems (the used taxonomy is depicted in Figure 1). Static trust based schemes rely on stable and preexisting relationships between peers, while dynamic trust is relying on a realtime assessment of peer behavior.

Other taxonomies have been proposed. [82] classifies cooperation enforcement mechanisms into trust-based patterns and trade-based patterns. Obreiter et al. distinguish between static trust, thereby referring to pre-established trust between peers, and dynamic trust, by which they refer to reputation-based trust. They analyze trade-based patterns as being based either on immediate or on deferred remuneration. Other authors describe cooperation in self-organized systems only in terms of reputation based and remuneration based approaches. Trust establishment, a further step in many protocols, easily maps to reputation but may rely on remuneration as well. In this work, we adhere to the existing classification of cooperation incentives in distinguishing between reputation-based and remuneration-based approaches.

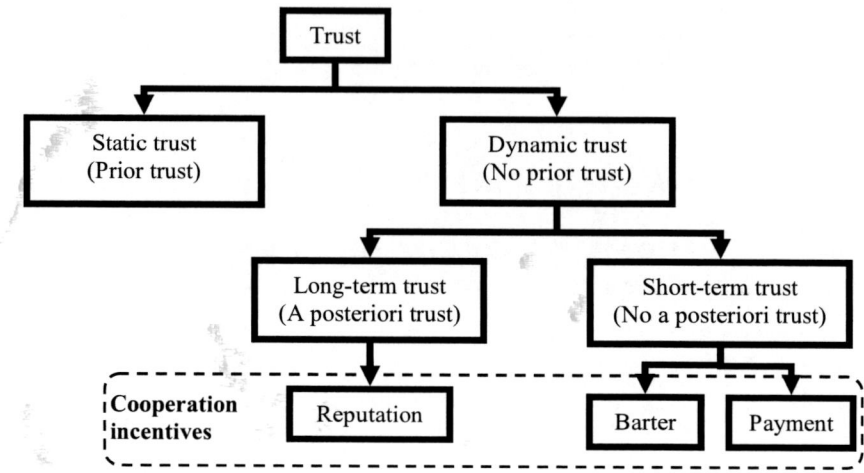

Figure 1. Trust taxonomy.

A. Static Trust

Peers may have prior trust relationships based for example on existing social relationships or a common authority. In friend-to-friend (F2F) networks, peers only interact and make direct connections with people they know. Passwords or digital signatures can be used to establish secure connections. The shared secrets needed for this are agreed-upon by out-of-band means. Turtle [14] is an anonymous information sharing system that builds a P2P overlay on top of pre-existent friendship relations among peers. All direct interactions occur between peers who are assumed to trust and respect each other as friends. Friendship relations are defined as commutative, but not transitive.

[43] proposes a F2F storage system where peers choose their storage sites among peers that they trust instead of randomly. Compared to an open P2P storage system, the proposed approach reduces the replication rate of the stored data since peers are only prone to failure not to departure or misbehavior. However, the approach is more applicable to certain types of storage systems like backup since it provides data durability not generally data

availability: peers may not often leave the system but they me be offline. F2F-based approaches ensures the cooperation of peers which results in enhanced system stability and reduces administrative overhead; even though these approaches does not help to build large scale systems with large reserve of resources.

B. Dynamic Trust

The P2P storage system may rely on the cooperation of peers without any prior trust relationships. The trust is then established during peer interactions through cooperation incentive mechanisms. Peers trust each other either gradually based on reputation or explicitly through bartered resources or payment incentives. The lack of prior trust between peers allows building open large scale systems that are accessible to the public. Storage systems with cooperation incentives perhaps result in more overhead than with prior trust based approaches; but however the reliability of the stored data is increased since data will be generally stored in multiple copies at different worldwide locations rather than confined at one or limited number of locations.

Peers choose to contribute or not to the storage system. The evaluation of each peer behavior allows determining the just incentives to stimulate its cooperation. In their turn, such incentives guide the peer in adapting its contribution level. The peer chooses the best strategy that maximizes its utility gained from the system: it compensates the cost incurred due to its potential contribution with the incentives received in support for its cooperation. With such a cyclic process, the system dynamically reaches the status of "full" cooperation between peers (thus resembling a system with static trust).

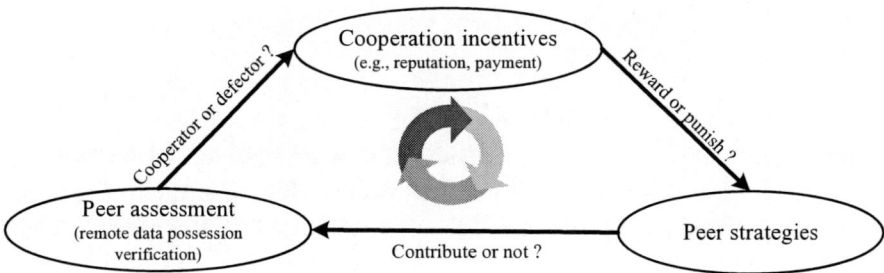

Figure 2. The feedback loop of dynamic trust.

Figure 2 depicts the feedback loop illustrating the correlation between peer assessment, cooperation incentives, and peer strategies.

1. Peer Assessment

Inciting peers to cooperate can only be achieved provided peer behavior is correctly assessed. Therefore, cooperation incentive mechanisms should comprise verification methods that measure the effective peer contributions in the P2P system.

An evaluation of the peer behavior can be performed at different timescales. An immediate evaluation of the peer behavior is only possible if the peer contribution occurs atomically like in packet forwarding application ([85] and [52]). Otherwise, peer evaluation is deferred to the completion of the peer contribution as in data storage. This constitutes a problem for storage applications where misbehaviong peers are left with an extensive period of time during which they can pretend to be storing some data they have in fact destroyed.

Periodic peer evaluation can be achieved through proof of knowledge protocols that have been called interchangeably remote data possession verifications, remote integrity verifications, proofs of data possession [33], or proofs of retrievability [8]. Such protocols are used as an interactive proof between the holder and the verifier or possibly the owner, in which the holder tries to convince the verifier that it possesses these very data without actually retrieving them. Interaction is based on challenge-response messages exchanged between the holder and the verifier. Verification of the holder's response is permitted through some information kept at the verifier side.

2. Cooperation Incentives

Peer behavior assessment forms the basis of an efficient cooperation incentive mechanism. From such evaluation, well-behaved peers will be rewarded with incentives while ill-behaved peers will be punished. Incentives may consist in exchanging identical resources (Barter), or in conferring good reputation to the well behaved peer, or in providing well behaved peers a financial counterpart for their cooperation.

Barter based approaches do not require the interacting peers to have any preset trust relationships. They rather rely on a simultaneous and reciprocal behavior. The exchange of resources takes place if both peers cooperate with each other; otherwise there is no exchange.

Reputation relies on the evaluation of the past behavior of a peer for deciding whether to cooperate with it. Reputation then builds a long-term trust between peers based on a statistical history of their past interactions. This allows going beyond barter-based approaches (direct reciprocity) by permitting to several peers to indirectly reciprocate to the behavior of the observed peer.

In contrast to reputation-based approaches, payment-based incentives constitute an explicit and discrete counterpart for cooperation and provide means to enforce a more immediate form of penalty for misconduct. Payment based approaches make it possible to secure short-term interactions between peers without relying neither on prior trust nor on some long-term history.

Chapter III

REMOTE DATA POSSESSION VERIFICATION

Self-organizing data storage must ensure data availability on a long term basis. This objective requires developing appropriate primitives for detecting dishonest peers free riding on the self-organizing storage infrastructure. Assessing such a behavior is the objective of data possession verification protocols. In contrast with simple integrity checks, which make sense only with respect to a potentially defective yet trusted server, verifying the remote data possession aims at detecting voluntary data destructions by a remote peer. These primitives have to be efficient: in particular, verifying the presence of these data remotely should not require transferring them back in their entirety; it should neither make it necessary to store the entire data at the verifier. The latter requirement simply forbids the use of plain message integrity codes as a protection measure since it prevents the construction of time-variant challenges based on such primitives.

A. Requirements

We consider a self-organizing storage application in which a peer, called the data *owner*, replicates its data by storing them at several peers, called data *holders*. The latter entities agree to keep data for a predefined period of time negotiated with the owner.

Peer behavior might be evaluated through the adoption of a routine check through which the holder should be periodically prompted to respond to a time-variant challenge as a proof that it holds its promise. Enforcing such a periodic verification of the data holder has implications on the performance and security of the storage protocol, which must fulfill requirements reviewed under the following two subsections.

1. Efficiency

The costs of verifying the proper storage of some data should be considered for the two parties that take part in the verification process, namely the verifier and the holder.

Storage Usage
The verifier must store a meta-information that makes it possible to generate a time-variant challenge based on the proof of knowledge protocol mentioned above for the verification of the stored data. The size of this meta-information must be reduced as much as possible even though the data being verified is very large. The effectiveness of storage at holder must also be optimized. The holder should store the minimum extra information in addition to the data itself.

Communication Overhead
The size of challenge response messages must be optimized. Still, the fact that the proof of knowledge has to be significantly smaller than the data whose knowledge is proven should not significantly reduce the security of the proof.

CPU Usage
Response verification and its checking during the verification process respectively at the holder and at the verifier should not be computationally expensive.

2. Security

The verification mechanism must address the following potential attacks which the data storage protocol is exposed to:

Detection of Data Destruction
The destruction of data stored at a holder must be detected as soon as possible. Destruction may be due to generic data corruption or to a faulty or dishonest holder.

Collusion-Resistance
Collusion attacks aim at taking unfair advantage of the storage application. There is one possible attack: replica holders may collude so that only one of them stores data, thereby defeating the purpose of replication to their sole profit.

Denial-of-Service (Dos) Prevention
DoS attacks aim at disrupting the storage application. DoS attacks may consist of flooding attacks, whereby the holder may be flooded by verification requests. The verifier may also be subject to similar attacks. They may also consist of Replay attacks, whereby a valid challenge or response message is maliciously or fraudulently repeated or delayed so as to disrupt the verification.

Man-in-the-Middle Attack Prevention
The attacker may pretend to be storing data to an owner without using any local disk space. The attacker simply steps between the owner and the actual holder and passes challenge-response messages back and forth, leaving the owner to believe the attacker is storing its data, when in fact another peer, the actual holder, stores the owner's data. The replication may again be disrupted with this attack: since the owner may run the risk of storing the data in two replicas at the same holder.

B. Verification Protocols

The verification protocol is an interactive check that may be formulated as a proof of knowledge [2] in which the holder attempts to convince a verifier that it possesses some data, which is demonstrated by correctly responding to queries that require computing on the very data.

The security of P2P storage applications has been increasingly addressed in recent years, which has resulted in various approaches to the design of storage verification primitives. The literature distinguishes two main categories of verification schemes: probabilistic ones that rely on the random checking of portions of stored data and deterministic ones that check the conservation of a remote data in a single, although potentially more expensive operation. Additionally, some schemes may authorize only a bounded number of verification operations conducted over the remote storage; yet the majority of schemes are designed to overcome this limitation.

Memory Checking

A potential premise of probabilistic verification schemes originates from memory checking protocols. A memory checker aims at detecting any error in the behavior of an unreliable data structure while performing the user's operations. The checker steps between the user and the data structure. It receives the input user sequence of "store" and "retrieve" operations over data symbols that are stored at the data structure. The checker checks the correctness of the output sequence from the structure using its reliable memory (noninvasive checker) or the data structure (invasive checker) so that any error in the output operation will be detected by the checker with high probability. In [54], the checker stores hash values of the user data symbols at its reliable memory. Whenever, the user requests to store or retrieve a symbol, the checker computes the hash of the response of the data structure and compares it with the hash value stored, and it updates the stored hash value if the user requested to store a symbol. The job of the memory checker is to recover and to check responses originating from an unreliable memory, not to check the correctness of the whole stored data. With the checker, it is possible to detect corruption of one symbol (usually one bit) per user operation.

Authenticator

The work of [65] better comprehends the remote data possession problem. It extends the memory checker model by making the verifier checks the consistency of the entire document in encoded version in order to detect if the document has been corrupted beyond recovery. The authenticator encodes a large document that will be stored at the unreliable memory and constructs a small fingerprint that will be stored at the reliable memory. Using the fingerprint, the authenticator verifies whether from the encoding it is possible to recover the document without actually decoding it. The authors of [65] propose a construction of the authenticator where there is a public encoding of the document consisting of index tags of this form: $t_i = f_{seed}(i \; o \; y_i)$ for each encoded value bit y_i having f_{seed} a pseudorandom function with *seed* taken as secret encoding. The authenticator is repeatedly used to verify for a selection of random indices if the tags correspond to the encoding values. The detection of document corruption is then probabilistic but improved with the encoding process of the document. Moreover, the query complexity is proportional to the number of indices requested. [77] proposes a similar solution to [65] but that achieves open verifiability i.e., the task of verifying data can be handed out to the public. The index tags are formulated as chunk signatures that the verifier keeps their corresponding public key. Signatures are indeed generated by the data owner; though the role of the verifier can be carried out by this latter or any peer that possesses the public key.

Provable Data Possession

The PDP (Provable Data Possession) scheme in [33] improves the authenticator model by presenting a new form of fingerprints $t_i=(hash(v\|i) \cdot g^{v_i})^d$ mod N, where $hash$ is a one-way function, v a secret random number, N an RSA modulus with d being a signature key, and g a generator of the cyclic group of $\mathbb{Z}_N^*$. With such homomorphic verifiable tags, any number of tags chosen randomly can be compressed into just one value by far smaller in size than the entire set, which means that communication complexity is independent of the number of indices requested per verification.

Proof of Retrievability

The POR protocol (Proof of Retrievability) in [8] explicitly expresses the question of data recovery in the authenticator problem: if the unreliable data passes the verification, the user is able to recover the original data with high probability. The protocol is based on verification of sentinels which are random values independent of the owner's data. These sentinels are disguised among owner's data blocks. The verification is probabilistic with the number of verification operations allowed being limited to the number of sentinels.

Compact Proofs of Retrievability

[39] improves the POR protocol by considering compact tags (comparable to PDP) that are associated with each data chunk y_i having the following form: $t_i = \alpha y_i + s_i$ where α and s_i are random numbers. The verifier requests random chunks from the unreliable memory and obtains a compact form of the chunks and their associated tags such that it is able to check the correctness of these tags just using α and the set $\{s_1, s_2, ...\}$ that are kept secret.

Remote Integrity Check

Remote Integrity Check of [22] alleviates the issue of data recovery and rather focuses on the repetitive verification of the integrity of the very data. The authors described several schemes some of them being hybrid construction of the existing schemes that fulfill the later requirement. For instance, the unreliable memory may store the data along with a signature of the data based on redactable signature schemes. With these schemes, it is possible to derive the signature of a chunk from the signature of the whole data, thus allowing the unreliable memory to compute the signature of any chunk requested by the verifier.

Data Chunk Recovery

The majority of the probabilistic verification schemes require the recovery of one or multiple (in plain or compacted form) data chunks. For example, in the solution of [55], the owner periodically challenges its holders by requesting a block out of the stored data. The response is checked by comparing it with the valid block stored at the owner's disk space. Another approach using Merkle trees is proposed by Wagner and reported in [84]. The data stored at the holder is expanded with a Merkle hash tree on data chunks and the root of the tree is kept by the verifier. It is not required from the verifier to store the data, on the contrary of [55]. The verification process checks the possession of one data chunk chosen randomly by the verifier that also requests a full path in the hash tree from the root to this random chunk.

Algebraic Signatures

The scheme proposed in [92] relies on algebraic signatures. The verifier requests algebraic signatures of data blocks stored at holders, and then compares the parity of these signatures with the signature of the parity blocks stored at holders too. The main drawback of the approach is that if the parity blocks does not match, it is difficult (depends on the number of used parity blocks) and computationally expensive to recognize the faulty holder.

Incremental Cryptography

First step toward a solution to the deterministic verification problem comes from incremental cryptographic algorithms that detect changes made to a document using a tag, a small secret stored at a reliable memory that relates to the complete stored document and that is quickly updatable if the user makes modifications. [63] proposes several incremental schemes where the tag is either an XORed sum of randomized document symbols or a leaf in a search tree as a result of message authentication algorithm applied to each symbol. These schemes provide tamper-proof security of the user document in its entirety; although they require recovering the whole data which is not practical for remote data verification because of the high communication overhead.

Deterministic Remote Integrity Check

The first solution described in [98] allows the checking of the integrity of the remote data, with low storage and communication overhead. It requires pre-computed results of challenges to be stored at the verifier, where a challenge corresponds to the hashing of the data concatenated with a random number. The protocol requires small storage at the verifier, yet they allow only a fixed number of challenges to be performed. Another simple deterministic approach with unlimited number of challenges is proposed in [32] where the verifier like the holder is storing the data. In this approach, the holder has to send the MAC of data as the response to the challenge message. The verifier sends a fresh nonce (a unique and randomly chosen value) as the key for the message authentication code: this is to prevent the holder peer from storing only the result of the hashing of the data.

Storage Enforcing Commitment

The SEC (Storage Enforcing Commitment) scheme in [84] aims at allowing the verifier to check whether the data holder is storing the data with storage overhead and communication complexity that are independent of the length of the data. Their deterministic verification approach uses the following tags that are kept at the holder along with the data: $PK=(g^x, g^{x^2}, g^{x^3}, ..., g^{x^n})$ where PK is the public key (stored at the holder) and x is the secret key (stored at the verifier). The tags are independent of the stored data, but their number is equal to two times the number of data chunks. The verifier chooses a random value that will be used to shift the indexes of tags to be associated with the data chunks when constructing the response by the holder.

Homomorphic Hash Functions

The second solution described in [98] requires little storage at the verifier side and no additional storage overhead at the holder side; yet makes it possible to generate an unlimited number of challenges. The proposed solution (inspired from RSA) has been also proposed by Filho and Barreto in [19]. It makes use of a key-based homomorphic hash function H. A construction of H is also presented as $H(m)=g^m \mod N$ where N is an RSA modulus and such that the size of the message m is larger than the size of N. In each challenge of this solution, a nonce is generated by the verifier which the prover combines with the data using H to prove the freshness of the answer. The prover's response will be compared by the verifier with a value computed over H(data) only, since the secret key of the verifier allows the following operation (d for data, and r for nonce): $H(d + r) = H(d) \times H(r)$. The exponentiation operation used in the RSA solution makes the whole data as an exponent. To reduce the computing time of verification, Sebé et al. in [25] propose to trade off the computing time required at the prover against the storage required at the verifier. The data is split in a number m of chunks $\{d_i\}_{1 \leq i \leq m}$, the verifier holds $\{H(d_i)\}_{1 \leq i \leq m}$ and asks the prover to compute a sum function of the data chunks $\{d_i\}_{1 \leq i \leq m}$ and m random numbers $\{r_i\}_{1 \leq i \leq m}$ generated from a new seed handed by the verifier for every challenge. Here again, the secret key kept by the verifier allows this operation: $\sum_{1 \leq i \leq m} H(d_i + r_i) = \sum_{1 \leq i \leq m} H(d_i) \times H(r_i)$. The index m is the ratio of tradeoff between the storage kept by the verifier and the computation performed by the prover. Furthermore, the basic solution can be still improved as described in [22]; though the verification method is probabilistic. The holder will be storing tags of $t_i = g^{y_i + s_i}$ where s_i is a random number kept secret by the verifier. The holder periodically constructs compact forms of the data chunks and corresponding tags using time-variant challenge sent by the verifier. The authors of [22] argue that this solution achieves a good performance.

C. DELEGABLE VERIFICATION PROTOCOL

Self-organization addresses highly dynamic environments like P2P networks in which peers frequently join and leave the system: this assumption implies the need for the owner to delegate data storage evaluation to third parties, termed *verifiers* thereafter, to ensure a periodic evaluation of holders after his leave. The need for scalability also pleads for distributing the verification function, in particular to balance verification costs among several entities. Last but not least, ensuring fault tolerance means preventing the system from presenting any single point of failure: to this end, data verification should be distributed to multiple peers as much as possible; data should also be replicated to ensure their high availability, which can only be maintained at a given level if it is possible to detect storage defection.

1. Delegability

The authenticator and the memory checker perform verifications on behalf of the user; though they are considered as trusted entities within the user's platform. None of the presented schemes considers distributing the verification task to other untrusted peers; they instead rely on the sole data owner to perform such verifications. In a P2P setting, it is important that the owner delegates the verification to other peers in the network in order to tolerate the intermittent connection of peers and even the fact that a single point of verification constitutes a single point of failure. Some of the schemes presented above may allow delegating verification provided that the verifier is not storing any secret information because it may otherwise collude with the holder. Additionally, the amortized storage overhead and communication complexity should be minimized for this purpose. To our knowledge, [78] is the first work to suggest delegating the verification task to multiple peers selected and appointed by the data owner. This approach relies on elliptic curve cryptography primitives., The owner derives from the data to be stored a public and condensed verification information expressed as $(d \mod N_n) \times P$ where N_n is the order of the elliptic curve and P is a generator. The interactive proof of knowledge exchange between the verifier and the holder is based on the hardness of the elliptic curve discrete logarithm problem [72]. Such a verification protocol can be further refined by considering data chunks instead of a data bulk in analogy to [25]. The objective in this case is to limit the computation overhead required from the holder. A revised verification protocol is described in more detail in the following sub-section.

The main characteristics of the discussed verification protocols are summarized in Table 1.

Table 1. Comparison of existing verification protocols (variable n and m respectively correspond to data size and the number of chunks).

	Detection	Delegation	Efficiency		
			Storage at verifier	CPU at holder	Communication overhead
[8]: POR	Probabilistic Bounded	No	$O(1)$	$O(1)$ hash transformation	$O(1)$
[54]: Memory checker	Probabilistic Unbounded	No	$O(m)$	$O(n/m)$ chunk fetching	$O(n/m)$

Table1. Continued.

	Detection	Delegation	Efficiency		
			Storage at verifier	CPU at holder	Communication overhead
[65]: Authenticator	Probabilistic Unbounded	No	$O(1)$	$O(n/m)$ chunk fetching	$O(n/m)$
[77]: based on signatures	Probabilistic Unbounded	Yes	$O(1)$	$O(n/m)$ chunk fetching	$O(n/m)$
[33]: PDP	Probabilistic Unbounded	Possible	$O(1)$	$O(n/m)$ exponentiation	$O(1)$
[39]: Compact proofs of retrievability	Probabilistic Unbounded	No	$O(1)$	$O(n/m)$ exponentiation	$O(1)$
[22]: based on redactable signatures	Probabilistic Unbounded	Possible	$O(1)$	$O(\log(n))$ signature construction	$O(\log(n))$
[22]: RSAh solution	Probabilistic Unbounded	No	$O(1)$	$O(n/m)$ exponentiation	$O(1)$
[55]: Data chunk recovery	Probabilistic Unbounded	No	$O(n)$	$O(1)$ simple comparison	$O(1)$
Wagner in [84]: based on Merkle-hash tree	Probabilistic Unbounded	Possible	$O(1)$	$O(\log(n))$ hash transformation	$O(\log(n))$
[92]: based on algebraic signatures	Probabilistic Unbounded	Possible	$O(1)$	$O(n/m)$ signature validation	$O(1)$
[98]: pre-computed challenges	Deterministic Bounded	No	$O(1)$	$O(n)$ hash transformation	$O(1)$
[63]: Incremental cryptography	Deterministic Unbounded	Possible	$O(1)$	$O(n)$ fetching	$O(n)$
[32]: MAC based	Deterministic Unbounded	No	$O(n)$	$O(n)$ hash transformation	$O(1)$
[84]: SEC	Deterministic Unbounded	No	$O(1)$	$O(n/m)$ exponentiation	$O(1)$
[98], [19]: RSA solution	Deterministic Unbounded	Possible	$O(1)$	$O(n)$ exponentiation	$O(1)$
[25]: RSA solution with data chunks	Deterministic Unbounded	Possible	$O(m)$	$O(n/m)$ exponentiation	$O(1)$
[78]: ECC based	Deterministic Unbounded	Yes	$O(m)$	$O(n/m)$ point multiplication	$O(1)$

2. Example

The following presents a secure and self-organizing verification protocol exhibiting a low resource overhead. This protocol was designed with scalability as an essential objective: it enables generating an unlimited number of verification challenges from the same small-sized security metadata.

a. Security Background

The deterministic verification protocol relies on elliptic curve cryptography ([72], [94]). The security of the protocol is based on two different hard problems. First, given some required conditions, it is hard to find the order of an elliptic curve. Furthermore, one of the most common problems in elliptic curve cryptography is the Elliptic Curve discrete logarithm problem denoted by ECDLP.

Thanks to the hardness of these two problems, the deterministic verification protocol ensures that the holder must use the whole data to compute the response for each challenge. In this section, we formalize these two problems in order to further describe the security primitives that rely on them.

Elliptic Curves over $\mathbb{Z}_n$. Let n be an odd composite square free integer and let a, b be two integers in $\mathbb{Z}_n$ such that $\gcd(4a^3 + 27b^2, n) = 1$ ("gcd" means greatest common divisor).

An elliptic curve $E_n(a, b)$ over the ring $\mathbb{Z}_n$ is the set of the points $(x, y) \in \mathbb{Z}_n \times \mathbb{Z}_n$ satisfying the equation: $y^2 = x^3 + ax + b$, together with the point at infinity denoted O_n.

Solving the Order of Elliptic Curves

The order of an elliptic curve over the ring $\mathbb{Z}_n$ where $n=pq$ is defined in [47] as $N_n = \text{lcm}(\#E_p(a, b), \#E_q(a, b))$ ("lcm" for least common multiple, "#" means order of). N_n is the order of the curve, i.e., for any $P \in E_n(a, b)$ and any integer k, $(k \times N_n + 1)P = P$.

If ($a = 0$ and $p \equiv q \equiv 2 \mod 3$) or ($b = 0$ and $p \equiv q \equiv 3 \mod 4$), the order of $E_n(a, b)$ is equal to $N_n=\text{lcm}(p+1, q+1)$. We will consider for the remainder of the paper the case where $a = 0$ and $p \equiv q \equiv 2 \mod 3$. As proven in [47], given $N_n = \text{lcm}(\#E_p(a, b), \#E_q(a, b)) = \text{lcm}(p + 1, q + 1)$, solving N_n is computationally equivalent to factoring the composite number n.

The Elliptic Curve Discrete Logarithm Problem

Consider K a finite field and $E(K)$ an elliptic curve defined over K. ECDLP in K is defined as: given two elements P and $Q \in K$, find an integer r, such that $Q = rP$ whenever such an integer exists.

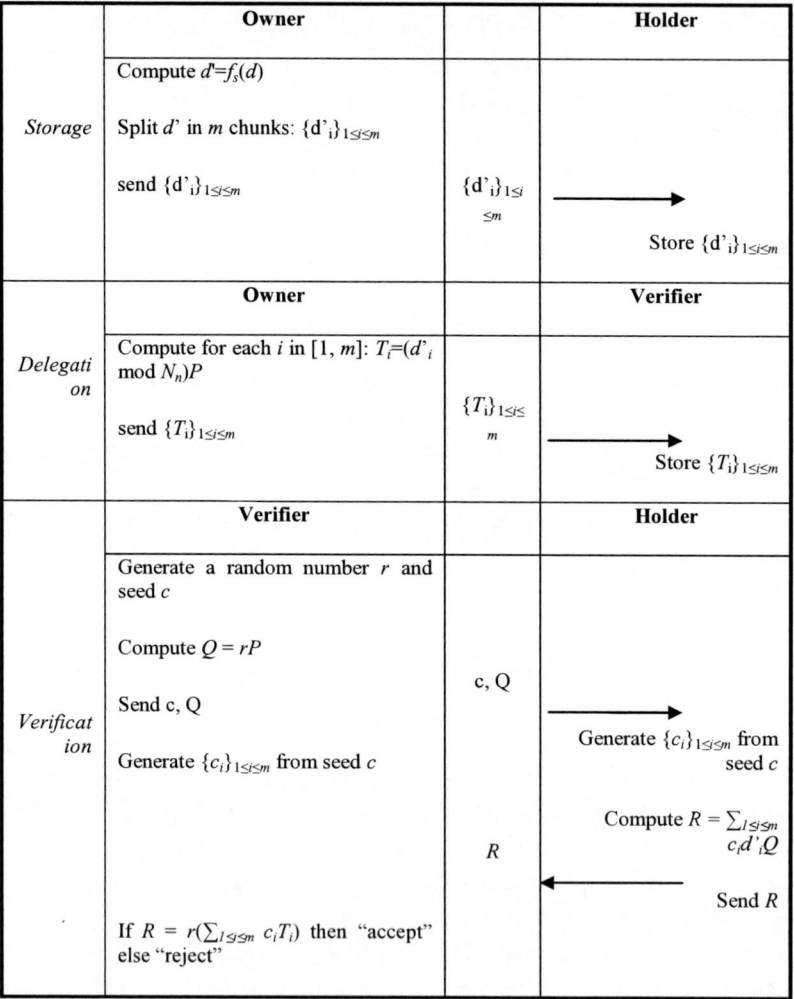

Figure 3. Delegable verification protocol.

b. Protocol Description

This sub-section introduces an improved version of the protocol described in [78] whereby the computation complexity at the holder is reduced. In the proposed version and in comparison to the version of [78], the data is split into m chunks, denoted $\{d'_i\}_{1\leq i\leq m}$, and the verifier stores the corresponding elliptic curve points $\{T_i = d'_i P\}_{1\leq i\leq m}$. We assume that the size of each data chunk is much larger than $4k$ where k is the security parameter that specifies the size of p and q and thus also the size of an elliptic curve point in $\mathbb{Z}_n$ ($n=pq$), because the verifier must keep less information than the full data.

The verification protocol is specified by four phases (see Figure 3): Setup, Storage, Delegation, and Verification. The owner communicates the data to the holder at the storage phase and the meta-information to the verifier at the delegation phase. At the verification phase, the verifier checks the holder's possession of data by invoking an interactive process. This process may be executed an unlimited number of times.

- *Setup:* The phase is performed by the owner. From a chosen security parameter k ($k > 512$ bits), the owner generates two large primes p and q of size k both congruent to 2 modulo 3, and computes their product $n = pq$. Then, it considers an elliptic curve over the ring $\mathbb{Z}_n$ denoted by $E_n(0, b)$ where b is an integer such that $\gcd(b, n)=1$, to compute a generator P of $E_n(0, b)$. The order of $E_n(0, b)$ is $N_n = \text{lcm}(p+1, q+1)$. The parameters b, P, and n are published and the order N_n is kept secret by the owner.

- *Storage:* The owner personalizes the data d for its intended holder using a keyed encryption function f_s, then splits the personalized data $d'= f_s(d)$ into m chunks of the same size (the last chunk is padded with zeroes): $\{d'_i\}_{1\leq i\leq m}$. The data chunks are then sent to the holder.

- *Delegation:* The owner generates meta-information to be used by the verifier for verifying the data possession of one holder. The owner generates the curve points $\{T_i = d'_i P \in E_n(0, b)\}_{1\leq i\leq m}$ sent to the verifier.

- *Verification:* The verifier generates a random number r and a random seed c (size of $c > 128$ bits). Then, it sends $Q=rP$ and the seed c to the holder. Upon reception of this, the holder generates m random numbers $\{c_i\}_{1\leq i\leq m}$ from the seed c (it is possible to generate the random numbers as $c_i=c^i$ for each i, or using a random number generator function). Then, it computes the point $R = \sum_{1\leq i\leq m} c_i d'_i Q$ that is sent to the verifier. To decide whether holder's proof is accepted or rejected, the verifier generates the same m random numbers $\{c_i\}_{1\leq i\leq m}$ from the seed c and checks if R is equal to $r(\sum_{1\leq i\leq m} c_i T_i)$.

c. Security Analysis

This section analyzes the completeness and the soundness of the deterministic protocol that are the two essential properties of a proof of knowledge protocol [2]: a protocol is complete if, given an honest claimant and an honest verifier, the protocol succeeds with overwhelming probability, i.e., the verifier accepts the claimant's proof; a protocol is sound if, given a dishonest claimant, the protocol fails, i.e. the claimant's proof is rejected by the verifier, except with a small probability.

Theorem 1- The proposed protocol is complete: if the verifier and the holder correctly follow the proposed protocol, the verifier always accepts the proof as valid.

Proof: Thanks to the commutative property of point multiplication in an elliptic curve, we have for each i in $[1, m]$: $d'_i rP = rd'_i P$. Thus, the equation: $\sum_{1\leq i\leq m} c_i d'_i rP = r(\sum_{1\leq i\leq m} c_i d'_i P)$. □

Theorem 2- The proposed protocol is sound: if the claimant does not store the data, then the verifier will not accept the proof as valid.

Proof: If the holder does not store the data chunks $\{d'_i\}_{1\leq i\leq m}$, it may try first to collude with other holders storing the same data. However, this option is not feasible since data stored at each holder is securely personalized during the storage phase. Since f_s is a keyed encryption function and the key s is secret, no peer except the owner can retrieve the original data d from d'. The other way to generate a correct response without storing the data relies on only storing $\{d'_i P\}_{1\leq i\leq m}$ (which is much smaller than the full data size) and retrieving r from the challenge rP in order to compute the correct response. Finding r is hard based on ECDLP. The last option for the holder to cheat is to keep $\{d'_i \bmod N_n\}_{1\leq i\leq m}$ instead of d' (whose size is very large). The holder cannot compute N_n based on the hardness of solving the order of $E_n(0, b)$. Thus, if the response is correct then the holder keeps the data correctly. □

d. Performance Analysis

In the proposed protocol, challenge-response messages mainly each consist of an elliptic curve point in $\mathbb{Z}_n^2$. Message size is thus a function of the security factor k (size of $n \approx 2k$). Reducing communication overhead then means decreasing the security parameter.

The verification protocol requires the verifier to store a set of elliptic curve points that allows producing on demand challenges for the verification. Finally, the creation of proof and its verification rely on point multiplication operations.

The number of data chunks m can be used to fine tune the ratio between the storage required at the verifier and the computation expected from the holder: when increasing m, the verifier is required to keep more information for the verification task, but at the same time the holder is required to perform one point multiplication operation using much smaller scalars.

Assessing the actual state of storage in a P2P storage application represents the first step towards efficiently reacting to misbehavior and cooperation incentives rely on peer evaluations. The use of verification protocols should make it possible to detect and isolate selfish and malicious peers, and ultimately punish these peers through cooperation incentive mechanisms.

Table 2. Summary of resource usage of the delegable verification protocol (variable n and m respectively correspond to data size and the number of chunks).

	Storage usage	Computation complexity	Communication overhead
At holder	$O(n)$	$O(n/m)$	(upstream) $O(1)$
At verifier	$O(m)$	$O(1)$	(upstream) $O(1)$

Chapter IV

COOPERATION INCENTIVES

Cooperation enforcement is a central feature of P2P systems, and even more so self-organizing systems, to compensate for the lack of a dedicated and trusted coordinator and still get some work done. However, cooperation to achieve some functionality is not necessarily an objective of peers that are not under the control of any authority and that may try to maximize the benefits they get from the P2P system. Cooperation incentive schemes have been introduced to stimulate the cooperation of such self-interested peers. They are diverse not only in terms of the applications which they protect, but also in terms of the features they implement, the type of reward and punishment used, and their operation over time. Cooperation incentives are classically classified into barter-based, reputation-based, and remuneration-based approaches.

A. Bartering

Cooperation incentives may be cheaply built on a tit-for-tat (TFT) strategy ("give and ye shall receive"). The peer initially cooperates, and then responds likewise to the opponent's previous action: if the opponent previously cooperated, the peer cooperates; otherwise, the peer defects. TFT is demonstrated to be an evolutionary stable strategy (ESS) in game theory jargon: this strategy cannot be invaded (or dominated) by any alternative yet initially rare strategy.

In the Cooperative Internet Backup Scheme [55], each peer has a set of geographically-separated partner peers that collectively hold its backed up data. In return, the peer backs up a part of its partners' data. To detect free-riding, each peer periodically evaluates its remote data. If it detects that one of its partners dropped the data, the peer establishes a backup contract with a different partner. Since the scheme relies on identical and immediate resource exchanges, peers must be able to choose partners that match their needs and their capabilities and that ensure similar uptimes. To this end, a central server tracks peers and their partners. Decentralized methods of finding partners in a Gnutella-like flooding approach are also suggested although not evaluated in [55].

However, TFT is not perfect as illustrated by the P2P file sharing protocol BitTorrent [13]. In BitTorrent, unchoking a peer means that the peer is accepted to upload files for it. Peers follow a TFT strategy by unchoking peers that provide the highest throughput for them, and besides that they use an optimistic unchoking strategy to discover potentially better trading peers. However this strategy of (probabilistically) cooperating with newcomers blindly can be exploited by whitewashers (peers that repeatedly join the network under new identities to avoid the penalty imposed on free-riders). [58] describes the design of BitTyrant, a selfish client that demonstrates that BitTorrent incentives don't build robustness. The reason is that TFT is no longer an evolutionary stable strategy in the presence of whitewashers.

B. Reputation

Reputation relies on the evaluation of a peer's past behavior for deciding whether to cooperate with the peer. Cooperation may be reciprocated even in the absence of its beneficiary and evaluator (indirect reciprocity).

Direct Vs. Indirect Reputation

Reputation generally only relies on a partial assessment of the behavior of peers, which might delay the detection of free-riders. This situation is rendered even worse in P2P storage applications, since storage is not an instantaneous operation and data are vulnerable throughout their entire storage lifetime. Group-based architecture have been suggested (e.g., [75]) as a way to enable peers to quickly know the behavior of their group fellows. The analytical model in [75] compares direct reputation whereby peers use only the results of verifications they perform themselves using direct observations to compute reputation with indirect reputation where these results are disseminated. This model demonstrates that the direct reputation approach for observing peer behavior outperforms indirect reputation in terms of correctness and exposure if the group of peers is of modest size. However, indirect reputation is more effective in an open system with a large population of peers that have asymmetric interests as shown in [61].

The direct reputation approach does not require propagating any information as opposed to indirect reputation which generates communication overhead and may even require centralization. However, it is possible to implement a decentralized indirect reputation for example on top of a distributed-hash-table (DHT) or by disseminating information to other peers similarly to routing protocols.

Resistance to Bashing

Another challenging issue in dynamic systems like P2P is the vulnerability of a reputation system to peer bashing. Reputation bashing is made possible with two types of attacks: peer collusion and Sybil attacks. Peers may collude in order to advertise their quality more than their real values ("ballot stuffing") thus increasing their reputation at other peers. Such an objective can also be achieved through a Sybil attack: if peers are able to generate new identities at will, they may use some of them to increase the reputation of the rest of their made-up identities.

Techniques to completely eliminate Sybil attacks can only be provided by trusted certification as proven by Douceur [45]. In this way, trusted devices associated in a secure fashion to peers can be used to eliminate such attacks (as discussed in [88]). However, an attacker may still buy multiple devices and then acquire multiple identities although at a high cost. Without a trusted infrastructure, Sybil attacks can only be mitigated.

To overcome the collusion problem, [31] proposes to add a "reliability" measure to the estimate of the reputation. The rating measure L becomes:

$$L = \alpha \times R + (1 - \alpha) \times (1 - G)$$

where R is the estimated reputation, G is the Gini coefficient that describes the amount of inequality in the distribution of transactions among a peer's entire partner set, α being a weight parameter. The Gini coefficient illustrates the idea that a reputation estimate is considered as less reliable if a significant fraction of transactions are performed with a small subset of the peer's partner set.

[61] addresses the same problem of peer collusion throught the application of the maxflow algorithm on the graph constructed from peers considered as vertices and the services they receive as directed edges. The maxflow

algorithm gives the maximum feasible flow from a source peer to a destination peer. The cost of the maxflow algorithm increases with the number of peers examined in the graph.

The two approaches above are still trading off the number of peers examined in the algorithms with the efficiency of the detection. Sybil mitigation can also be achieved by making the newcomer pay with computational or bandwidth or storage abilities, such as for example crypto-puzzles [95] or testing peer IP address. Other techniques like SybilGuard [37] rely on prior trust relationships, e.g., real-world friendship between peers to detect Sybil attackers. [26] even enhances the SybilGuard approach by controlling the number of peer invitations that a group member possesses. In a similar fashion, [76] suggests that peers taking part in any transaction be simply chosen in a random fashion. Peer service requests are directed to a randomly chosen peers although the latter can choose to cooperate with the requesters based on their reputation.

In most of the approaches above, the costs are only paid once by Sybil attackers and can be then amortized during the rest of the system operation. As discussed in [15], such costs can be periodically paid by repeatedly performing resource testing on peers thus confining the potential return on investment of Sybil attackers to a limited time slot. It should be noted though that all these approaches, which aim at limiting Sybil attacks without trusted infrastructure, are scalable compared with certification-based approaches. Still, they incur a huge cost overhead not only on Sybil attackers but also on honest newcomers, which may undermine their practicality and adoption in P2P applications. Furthermore, [60] shows that imposing a penalty on all newcomers significantly degrades system performance when the peer churn rate is high.

C. Payment

Payment is a way to foster cooperation in exchange of some token that can be exchanged later on for some service. This approach introduces economic mechanisms that can regulate the usage of storage or bandwidth related resources, for instance. Payment brings up new requirements regarding the fairness of payment itself [68], which in general translate to a more complex and costly implementation than for reputation mechanisms. In particular, payment schemes require a trusted environment including trusted entities such as banks. These entities may be involved in the transaction, in which case the payment scheme can be deemed centralized. On the contrary, some schemes are decentralized and require banks to be contacted only to resolve payment litigations. The latter approach is more appropriate to ensure the maximum degree of self-organization to the P2P network.

Fair Exchange and Payment

Achieving an effective implementation of payment-based mechanism depends upon the realization of a protocol that enforces the fair exchange of the payment (credits) against some task: according to [69], "*a fair exchange protocol can then be defined as a protocol that ensures that no player in an electronic commerce transaction can gain an advantage over the other player by misbehaving, misrepresenting or by prematurely aborting the protocol*". Fair exchange may be enforced through a trusted third party (TTP) that may be used online or opportunistically. Tamperproof modules (TPMs), secure operating systems, or smart cards may also be employed to carry out a fair exchange protocol in a distributed fashion.

In a P2P network, TTPs may be represented as super-peers that play the same role as an online TTP but in a distributed fashion. FastTrack [42] is an example of such an architecture which is used in P2P networks like KaZaA [46], Grokster [36], and iMesh [40]. These networks have two-tier hierarchy consisting of ordinary nodes (ONs) in the lower tier and super-nodes (SNs) in the upper tier. In P2P file sharing networks, SNs keep track of ONs and other SNs and act as directory servers during the search phase of files. One way of implementing a payment scheme is to use super-peers distributed within the P2P network. These super-peers then provide neutral platforms for performing an optimistic fair exchange protocol. The use of such an infrastructure of trusted peers, that would not necessarily need to be related with the payment authority, may be rendered feasible by the deployment of other infrastructures like content distribution networks (CDNs) (e.g., [1]). Such networks involve the deployment of managed workstations all over the Internet, thereby providing a nice platform for payment related functionalities.

The Wuala storage system ensures fair exchange through a system of quota that directly depends on the measure of the uptime of a peer. Fair exchange in this system is ensured by a central authority that keeps track of exchanges between peers. In contrast, P2P storage systems may have no dedicated authority tracking all exchanges. In that case, ensuring the scalability of the system makes it necessary to resort to a type of fair exchange protocol called optimistic [68] in which the TTP does not necessarily take part in peer interactions, but may be contacted to arbitrate litigations. In the cooperative backup system of [55], a central server considered as a TTP tracks the partners of each peer participating in the backup system. Each peer takes note of its direct experience with a partner, and if this partner does not cooperate voluntarily or not beyond some threshold, the peer may decide to establish a backup contract with a different partner that is obtained through the central server.

Smart cards have been used in the P2P storage system PAST [81] to ensure the fairness of peer contributions. Smart cards issued by a third party are held by each PAST peer to support a quota system that balances supply and demand of storage space in the system. Peers cannot use more remote storage than they are providing locally. With fixed quotas and expiration dates, peers are only allowed to use as much storage as they contribute.

If data storage should be achieved in a large-scale and open P2P system, deploying designs based on trusted environments may be infeasible. In that case, implementing the optimistic fair exchange protocol would have to be done by relying solely on peers. [69] describes design rules for such cryptographic protocols making it possible to implement appropriate fair-exchange protocols. For instance, the distribution of the banking function to multiple peers may make the realization of a scalable system easier. In the KARMA framework [95], the exchange of some payment against some resource is supported by multiple peers that collaborate to provide a fair exchange. A fair exchange system for P2P storage system might be implemented using that framework in which the bank (trusted authority) is replaced by a set of peers, termed the bank-set, randomly assigned for each peer. The karma values, which is the name of the currency, are maintained for each peer by its bank-set who is collectively responsible for continuously updating the karma value as the peer contributes and consumes resources from the P2P system. The bank-sets independently track the credits belonging to their assigned peers, and periodically agree on a given balance of credits with a majority rule. Even if there were inconsistencies in peers' balances, transactions among peers correspond to tiny micropayments and thus do not produce considerable gains or losses to peers. The fair exchange protocol in KARMA is similar to an online TTP-based exchange but with additional features for guaranteeing the consistence and synchronization of balances.

Payments by Installment

A payment scheme for a file sharing application as described in [95] cannot be assimilated to P2P storage since in the former case payments are immediately charged after the exchange of the file, whereas in the latter case payments for storage are by installment i.e., they are billed at a due date that corresponds to the confirmation (after a verification) of the cooperative behavior of the holder. A payment scheme should thus be supplemented by an escrowing mechanism to guarantee the effective payment of credits promised by the peers towards a cooperative holder. Before interacting with others, a peer must escrow, i.e., set aside and store in a trusted repository, the amount of credits it agrees to pay at the end of the interaction upon defined conditions. The escrowing is an additional mechanism required for implementing fair-exchange in P2P storage systems since the misbehavior of a peer and a related compensation may not be determined immediately, but only at a later time when the peer in question might have left the network or would not respond. Escrowed credits thus form a commitment for future payments. Here again, trusted environments like TPMs or smartcards may prove helpful to implement the escrowing feature. Otherwise, third parties have to be used in every protocol that might imply some form of monetary compensation.

Preventing Starvation

Payment-based schemes generally suffer from starvation, e.g., see [9]. In a P2P storage system, starvation means the inability of a peer to store data in the system because it cannot commit money for potential compensation. Auctions provide a solution for mitigating that starvation phenomenon. Since auctioning reveals the real preferences of bidders, a solution is to make it necessary for peers left with a small number of credits to contribute more to the system. These peers would offer lower prices for storing the same amount of data in order to attract data owners in priority. First-price or second-price auctions (Vickrey auction) are equally possible.

Chapter V

VALIDATION BASED ON GAME THEORY

Cooperation incentives prevent selfish behaviors whereby peers free-ride the storage system, that is, they store data onto other peers without contributing to the storage infrastructure. Remote data verification protocols are required to implement the auditing mechanism needed by any efficient cooperation incentive mechanism. In general, a cooperation incentive mechanism is proven to be effective if it is demonstrated that any rational peer will always choose to cooperate whenever it interacts with another cooperative peer. One-stage games or repeated games have been mostly used to validate cooperation incentives that describe individual strategies; in addition, the use of evolutionary dynamics can help describe the evolution of strategies within large populations.

A. Definitions

Game theory is a branch of applied mathematics that models interactions among individuals making decisions. It attempts to mathematically capture individual rational behavior in strategic situations where individuals' decisions are based on their preferences and also depend on the other individuals' choices. It then provides a language to describe, analyze, and understand strategic scenarios [91].

1. Game
A game consists of:

- A set of *players* {p_1, ..., p_n} which are the individuals who make decisions
- A set of *strategies* i.e., moves for each player S_i, $i=1, ..., n$
- A specification of each player's *payoffs* which are the numeric values assigned to the outcomes produced by the various combinations of strategies. Payoffs represent the preference ordering of players over the outcomes. Payoffs are expressed using player's *utility function* U_i:

$$U_i: S_1 \times S_2 \times ... \times S_n \rightarrow \Re$$

The game assumes that all players are *rational*; this means that they will always choose the strategy that maximizes their payoffs. Players are then participants in the game with the goal of choosing the actions that produce their most preferred outcomes.

2. Game Types

A game can be one of two types: *non-cooperative* or *cooperative*. In the first type, players are selfish and are only concerned with maximizing their own benefit. In the second type, some players cooperate and form a coalition in order to achieve a common goal, and then the coalition and the rest of players play non-cooperatively the game.

A game can be a *repeated game* that consists in a finite or infinite number of iterations of some one-stage game. In such one-stage game, players' choices are referred to as actions rather than strategies (a term reserved to the repeated game) and these actions take into account their impact on the future actions of other players.

Evolutionary game theory also provides a dynamic framework for analyzing repeated interactions. In such games, randomly chosen players interact with each other, then the player with the lower payoff switches to the strategy of the player with the higher payoff i.e., players reproduce proportionally to their payoffs. Hence, strategies with poor payoffs eventually die off, while well-performing strategies thrive.

3. Game Equilibria

Finding a solution to a game equates to finding equilibria in the game. At the equilibrium, each player of the game has adopted a strategy that they are unlikely to change. Many equilibrium related concepts have been developed in an attempt to capture this idea. The most famous is the *Nash equilibrium*. A

Nash Equilibrium is the set of players' strategy choices such that no player can benefit by changing its strategy while the other players keep their strategies unchanged. So, it is a set of strategies $\{\sigma_1 \in S_1, ..., \sigma_n \in S_n\}$, such that:

$$U_i(\sigma_1, ..., \sigma_i, ..., \sigma_n) \geq U_i(\sigma_1, ..., \sigma'_i, ..., \sigma_n), \forall i \in \{1, ..., n\} \text{ and } \sigma'_i \in S_i$$

An *Evolutionary stable strategy* (ESS) defines strategies conducting to a Nash equilibrium and such that, if adopted by a population of players, cannot be invaded by any alternative strategy that is initially rare. For a two-player game with a strategy space S, a strategy $\sigma*$ is an ESS if and only if for any $\sigma' \neq \sigma*$, either one of the following two conditions holds:

a) $U(\sigma*, \sigma*) > U(\sigma', \sigma*)$
b) $U(\sigma*, \sigma*) = U(\sigma', \sigma*)$ and $U(\sigma*, \sigma') > U(\sigma', \sigma')$

Here, $U(.,.)$ is the payoff function of the associated two-player game.

To achieve a socially optimal equilibrium for a self-organizing system with autonomous peers, different incentive mechanisms have been proposed in the literature. These incentives include providing virtual or real payment incentives or establishing and maintaining a reputation index for every peer in the network.

B. Reputation Incentive Modeling

The cooperation enforcement property of reputation schemes can be proven with game theoretical tools. The modeling may operate with static games that consider interaction between peers that have persistent strategies. On the other hand, dynamic games involve peers that constantly change their strategy. The following reviews static and dynamic game models that describe several features of reputation approaches.

1. Static games
Reputation schemes have received a great deal of attention for enforcing node cooperation in mobile ad hoc networks. Notably, [85] proposed CORE as a collaborative reputation mechanism motivating nodes to forward packets, and used a game theoretical approach to assess the features and validate the mechanism. This work relies on a cooperative game that uses a two-period structure: players first decide whether or not to join a coalition, and then both

the coalition and the remaining players choose their behavior non-cooperatively. Additionally, the model employs a preferential structure as suggested by the ERC-theory [30]. A player i's utility is based on the absolute payoff y_i and on the relative payoff:

$$\sigma_i = \frac{y_i}{\sum_j y_j}$$

The ERC utility function is derived then as:

$$U_i = \alpha_i u(y_i) + \beta_i r(\sigma_i)$$

where α_i and β_i are parameters describing the preferences of the nodes.

The study of the model demonstrates that there is a Nash equilibrium where at least half of the total number of nodes cooperate. Nodes may also have a continuous strategy space where they may choose their cooperation levels instead of discretely choosing just between cooperation and defection. The study reveals that for identical ERC preferences and for a sufficiently small ratio α/β (i.e., nodes are interested enough in being close to the equal share), then the grand coalition is stable, i.e., no player has an incentive to leave the coalition. Still, the assumption that the nodes will be much interested in their relative payoff (small α/β) may not be met in practice.

2. Dynamic games

In contrast to [85] that addresses a specific mechanism, [16] introduces a general game theoretical framework to model and analyze cooperation incentive policies, and to more specifically focus on their dynamics. In the proposed model, peer strategies are expressed using an $n \times n$ generosity matrix G with G_{ij} being the probability that a peer of strategy s_i will provide service for peer of strategy s_j. The expected payoff of a peer of strategy s_i at time t is derived as:

$$\bar{P}_i(t) = \sum_{j=1}^{n} x_j(t) \times (\alpha G_{ji} - G_{ij})$$

where $x_j(t)$ denotes the fraction of peers with strategy s_j in the peer population at time t, $\alpha > 0$ is the gain of a peer receiving a service from another peer, while it loses β (normalized payoff with $\beta = 1$) when it provides a service to another peer. Thus, the total expected performance of the system is:

$$\bar{P}(t) = x^T G x$$

with the vector $x = (x_1, x_2, \ldots, x_n)$.

Instead of game equilibria, the model studies the game dynamics where strategies change according to two learning models: the current-best (CBLM) and the opportunistic (OLM) learning models. In CBLM, each peer may switch to another strategy with probability γ_a (adapting rate). The peer chooses the strategy s_h that has the highest payoff. The peer of strategy s_i will switch to strategy s_h with probability $\gamma_s(\bar{P}_h(t) - \bar{P}_i(t))$, where γ_s represents the sensitivity rate to the performance gap. System dynamics are then expressed by the following equations:

$$\dot{x}_i = -\gamma x_i(\bar{P}_h(t) - \bar{P}_i(t)); \ \forall \ i \neq h$$
$$\dot{x}_h = \gamma(\bar{P}_h(t) - \bar{P}(t)); \ \gamma = \gamma_a \gamma_s \text{ (learning rate)}$$

In the second learning model OLM, each peer randomly chooses another peer as its *teacher* with probability γ_a. If the teacher has a better payoff than the peer, the latter adapts to the teacher's strategy with sensitivity γ_s to their performance gap. OLM is similar to evolutionary game concepts where the so-called teacher is the co-player of the peer. For this reason, the evolution of the system with OLM follows the replicator dynamics (the payoff is in number of offsprings):

$$\dot{x}_i = \gamma x_i(\bar{P}_i(t) - \bar{P}(t))$$

The main parameter of comparison between these learning models is robustness: a system is robust if it stays at a high contribution level despite perturbations such as peer arrivals or departures from the network. The mathematical analysis demonstrates that a system with CBLM is less robust than with OLM, the latter being akin to a typical evolutionary game model. Moreover, the analysis allows comparing two incentive policies. The first considered policy is the mirror incentive policy under which a peer provides service with the same probability as the requester serves other peers in the system. On the other hand, in a second policy named the proportional incentive policy, the peer serves the requester with a probability equal to the requester's contribution to consumption ratio. The study shows that the mirror incentive policy may lead to a complete system collapse, while the proportional incentive policy can lead to a robust system. This result is quite interesting because it demonstrates that a policy motivating fairness in terms of contributions and consumptions of resources achieves better stability than participatory incentives.

Another reputation technique to support cooperative behavior in a P2P system, named reciprocative strategy, is proposed in [61]. In this strategy, a peer j cooperates with another peer i depending on its normalized generosity value:

$$g_j(i) = \frac{g(i)}{g(j)}$$

where peer i's generosity $g(i) = p_i/c_i$, and p_i and c_i are respectively the services the peer i has provided and consumed. The reputation technique resembles the proportional incentive policy of [16], though the normalization overcomes the system bootstrapping problem.

To validate the reputation technique while taking into account several challenging issues of P2P systems such as their large populations, high turnover, asymmetry of interest of peers, and zero-cost identities, the authors propose a dynamic and asymmetric game model based on the generalized Prisoner's Dilemma (GPD). The dynamic model is composed of multiple rounds. In each round, every player plays a client role in one game, then a server role in another game. Every such player may subsequently either mutate by switching to a randomly picked strategy, or learn by switching to a strategy with a higher score determined by reputation, or turnover by leaving the system, or finally stay with the same strategy.

[48] also opted for an evolutionary study of applications in P2P systems. The authors proposed a model that they call a generalized form of the Evolutionary Prisoner's Dilemma (EPD). Though the model is very similar to the traditional EPD, they argue that the new model permits asymmetric transactions between a client peer and a server peer. The proposed model consists of several generations of rounds. At the end of a generation, the history of other players' actions is cleared and players evolve according to $r_i^{t+1} = r_i^t \times s_i^t$, where r_i^{t+1} is the frequency of peers playing strategy i at the $(t+1)^{th}$ generation, and r_i^t at the tth generation. s_i^t is their average score obtained after the tth generation. Peers decide whether to cooperate based on a reciprocative decision function that sets the probability to cooperate with a given peer X to the ratio (rounded to a value in [0, 1]):

$$\frac{cooperation\ X\ gave}{cooperation\ X\ received}$$

Such a function is comparable to the proportional incentive policy of [16] in which EPD is simulated under various situations. This work shows that techniques relying only on private history, where solely peer experiences are taken into account, fail in stimulating cooperation among peers as the population size increases. However, techniques based on a shared history scale better to large populations.

The evolutionary game proposed in [74] attempts to validate a large scale P2P storage system that is based on private history to estimate reputation. The reputation scheme relies on a verification routine to detect selfish behavior. Thus, peers may play several roles throughout the game: owner, holder, or verifier. In the proposed game inspired from the donor-recipient model of [38], the owner is considered a recipient, the r holders and m verifiers are donors. The owner gains b if at least one holder donates at a cost $-c$; however if no holder donates then the owner gains βb if at least one verifier donates at a cost $-\alpha c$ ($\alpha \leq 1$) for each verifier. The latter case corresponds to the situation where the cooperative verifier informs the owner of the data destruction, and then the owner may replicate its data elsewhere in the network thus maintaining the security properties of the stored data (e.g., the replication rate of the data).

Holders and verifiers have the choice between cooperating and defecting. The following peer strategies are specifically studied: altruistic peers that always donate, defectors that never donate and discriminators that donate under conditions. If the discriminator does not know its co-player, it will always donate; however, if it had previously played with its co-player, it will only donate if its co-player donates in the previous game. This strategy resembles Tit-For-Tat but differs from it in that both the owner (the donor) and its verifiers may decide to stop cooperating with the holder in the future.

The evolution of these strategies is analyzed using the replicator dynamics. The basic concept of replicator dynamics is that the growth rate of peers taking a strategy is proportional to the fitness acquired by the strategy. Thus, the strategy that yields more fitness than average for the whole system increases, and vice versa.

The study of the convergence of the system to equilibrium proves that there exist parameter values for which discriminators may win against free-riding defectors. Discriminators are not hopeless when confronting defectors, even if the latter may dominate altruists. At the equilibrium of the game, both discriminators and defectors may coexist if there is some churn in the system, otherwise discriminators will dominate. The number of verifiers increases the frequency of discriminators at the equilibrium whereas a costly storage or an increase of the replication rate reduce this frequency.

3. Whitewashing Problem

An inherent problem to a cooperation incentive mechanism implemented in a dynamic system where peers may join or leave at any time is the whitewashing problem. Whitewashers are peers that repeatedly misbehave then leave the storage system and come back with new identities thus escaping the punishment imposed by the incentive mechanism. The whitewashing problem is essentially due to the presence of free or cheap pseudonyms for peers. Therefore, countering the whitewashing attacks demands either the use of irreplaceable pseudonyms, e.g., through the assignment of strong identities by a central trusted authority, or requires imposing a penalty on all newcomers. The first solution reduces the decentralized nature of P2P systems and introduces a single point of failure. The second option requires defining the right penalty parameter for the system. The penalty corresponds to the best tradeoff for restricting whitewashers while encouraging newcomers to participate.

The simulation results of [48] demonstrate that cooperation with strangers fails to encourage cooperation in the presence of whitewashers. The authors thus propose an adaptive policy in which the probability of cooperation with strangers becomes equal to $p_C^{t+1} = (1-\mu) \times p_C^t + \mu \times C_t$ at time $t+1$, where $C_t=1$ if the last stranger cooperated and equal to 0 otherwise. Simulations validate the adaptive policy by demonstrating that incentives based on such a policy make the system converge to higher levels of cooperation.

[60] studies in more detail the whitewashing problem in P2P systems using a game theoretical model that particularly takes into account the heterogeneity of user behaviors. Indeed, each user is characterized by a type that reflects its willingness to contribute resources (its generosity level): users of type t_i will contribute if and only if $t_i > 1/x$ where x is the fraction of contributing users. The fraction of contributors is then determined by the solution to:

$$x = \text{Probability}(t_i > 1/x)$$

In order to sustain the system when the societal generosity is low (low x), punishment mechanisms against free-riding users are required. The proposed punishment mechanism consists in imposing a penalty on free-riding behavior with probability ($1-p$). The optimal value for the probability p is defined by the maximum performance obtained from the system. The authors express such a performance as:

$$W_{system} = (\alpha x^\beta - 1)(x + (1-x)(1-p)); \quad \alpha > 0 \text{ and } 0 < \beta \leq 1$$

where $Q = \alpha x^\beta$ is the maximum benefit received by each user, an increasing function of the number of contributors with diminishing returns. The performance of the system is maximized with $p = p^* \geq 1/\alpha$. Still, such a mechanism can be undermined by the availability of cheap pseudonyms through which a free-rider may choose to whitewash. To measure the effect of a whitewashing behavior, the authors compute the system performance at $p = p^*$ considering the cases of permanent identities and free identities, in addition to different turnover rates that represent user arrival and departure rates (arrivals and departures are assumed to be *type-neutral*, i.e., they do not alter the type distribution). This study demonstrates that the penalty mechanism is effective when both the societal generosity and the turnover rate are low; otherwise a notable societal cost due to whitewashing is experienced.

[73] studies the penalty mechanism described in [60] with the evolutionary game model of [74] by changing the strategy of discriminators such that the latter only cooperate probabilistically with strangers and also introducing whitewashers into the game. The study of the game equilibrium convergence demonstrates that discriminators are not hopeless in front of whitewashers and that they may even win over them provided system parameters are chosen sensibly. The fraction of discriminators in the system should in particular not be null initially, and the replication rate and the churn sensed in the system should not be too high.

The simulation results also show that there is an optimal probability p for the penalty mechanism that achieves a high social welfare for the whole P2P storage system. However, a non-zero welfare is only obtained if the whitewashing phenomena is restricted to a given fraction of defectors. For instance, if all defectors are whitewashing, discriminators are entirely eliminated and the system collapses. This result motivates the requirement to supplement the proposed penalty mechanism with other means that prevent or at least limit the whitewashing behavior such as controlling the peers that join the system using a cryptographic puzzle [95] or the payment of a membership fee. Another solution is to force or motivate peers to stay online a minimum amount of time in the system like in Wuala [97] ($1/w$ is then increased) because peer connection time must be taken into consideration.

The penalty mechanism adopted with strangers can be adaptive. The probability that a peer cooperates with a stranger is defined in [61] as p_s/c_s where p_s and c_s are respectively the number of services that strangers have provided and consumed. The results of the simulation of the dynamic game model show that a system with this strategy can ensure the cooperation of peers with a sufficiently low turnover.

c. Payment Incentive Modeling

One of the first studies that considered payment schemes in P2P systems is [83], which uses a game theoretical model to study the potential benefits of introducing micro-payment methods into centralized P2P file-sharing systems such as Napster. In such systems, the strategies have two independent actions in order to catch the asymmetric aspect of interactions between peers, which are also called agents: sharing, i.e., providing the service, and downloading, i.e., acquiring the service. Agent actions and other several considerations are put together into one utility function that is defined for each agent a_i as:

$$U_i = (f_i^{AD}(AD) + f_i^{NV}(NV) + f_i^{AL}(AL)) - (f_i^{DS}(DS) + f_i^{BW}(BW)) - FT$$

where variables AD, NV, AL, DS, BW, and FT respectively denote the amount of files the agent desires to download, the number of options from where the agent may download, the altruism derived from contributing to the system, the disk space used, the bandwidth used, and the financial transfer for using the system. Concerning functions f, they are arbitrary functions: each of them maps a variable to its financial value conferred by the agent. Relying on this theoretical model, the authors have analyzed the equilibrium solution for multiple situations. Without considering any incentives ($FT=0$) as it is the case with Napster and disregarding the altruism variable of agents' utility functions ($f_i^{AL}(AL)=0$), the outcome of the equilibrium analysis results in an unique equilibrium where nothing is shared and nothing can be downloaded. With some level of altruism in the system, all agents, both altruistic and free-rider, are unrestrained from downloading, the whole cost then weighing over the small number of altruistic agents. Therefore, the authors propose alternatives based on payment to overcome the free-riding problem. The first proposed payment scheme consists in charging agents for every download, and rewarding them for every upload. The result of the equilibrium analysis of the model with the payment scheme shows that there is one unique and strict equilibrium where agents are extensively sharing and downloading files. This result validates the payment scheme; still, the analysis does not take into account the fact that agents share diverse files and some of them may store files that are sufficiently rare thus unfairly receiving a large fraction of all the download requests for these files. For that reason, the authors propose a second payment-based alternative that continues to penalize downloads, but rewards agents in proportion to the amount of material they share rather than the number of uploads they provide. The equilibrium analysis of the model shows that two strict equilibria may be reached through either full file sharing or no sharing at all; in contrast, simulation experiments of the model demonstrate that the system converges to an equilibrium where all agents cooperate by sharing files.

[51] takes a different direction for defining peer utility function that relies on payment more than the model of [83] does. The authors of [51] model a P2P backup service as a non-cooperative game using an economic model that relies on the following user utility:

$$U_i(C_i^s, C_i^o, \epsilon_i) = V_i(C_i^s) - P_i(C_i^o) - \epsilon_i$$

where C_i^s is the capacity of data to be stored in the system and C_i^o is the capacity of the offered disk space. V_i gives the price the user is willing to pay and P_i gives the price it is willing to be paid for. The monetary compensation is denoted ϵ_i:

$$\epsilon_i = p^s C_i^s - p^o C_i^o$$

where p^s and p^o are unit prices. The authors define demand and supply functions, d_i and s_i, as:

$$d_i(p) = (V_i')^{-1}(p) \text{ and } s_i(p) = (P_i')^{-1}(p)$$

These functions follow a chosen common form:

$$d_i(p) = a_i \times p \text{ and } s_i(p) = b_i \times p$$

The parameters, a_i and b_i, associated with the demand and supply functions and characterizing the profile of each user, turn out to be playing a crucial role on justifying the use of a pricing scheme or imposed symmetry with respect to the optimal situation of the service that is maximizing the social welfare defined as:

$$W := \sum_i V_i(C_i^s) - P_i(C_i^o)$$

Indeed, the theoretical study of the economic model shows that if users are homogeneous in terms of a_i and b_i, then it is better to opt for imposed symmetric user contributions rather than a pricing scheme. However, for a heterogeneous user population, which is the general case in P2P networks, the use of a pricing scheme by which a monopoly is introduced to fix unit prices for buying and selling storage resources is validated. Still the involvement of the operator in fixing prices for a P2P backup reduces the social welfare of the system by ¼ times its maximum.

A P2P storage system purely self-organized that uses a probabilistic verification routine to detect selfish holders and that relies on a payment scheme to punish these holders is modeled as a Bayesian game in [79]. In this game, the information about the characteristics of other players is incomplete because the verification protocol allows only probabilistic detection; thus, nature is introduced as a player for modeling uncertainty. The owner is not informed about the holder's type, which may be either cooperative or selfish. Such situations that cannot be discriminated belong to the same so-called "set of information". The owner still can probabilistically determine the holder's type based on its prior beliefs: with every verification operation performed, it updates its beliefs according to Bayes' formula.

The one-stage game produces a Nash equilibrium in which the owner and the holder are not cooperative. However, the perfect Bayesian equilibrium results in the cooperation of both players for some defined conditions. The study of the repeated Bayesian game proves that the iteration of the game favors the cooperativeness of the holder as well as that of the owner. The study also identifies which actions the owner must follow for a given initial belief about the cooperativeness of the holder. Finally, the study reveals the expressions that parameters of the payment scheme (e.g., reward, punishment) should verify. [79] approaches the definition of payment parameters from a design theory point of view rather than a game theory approach in that it endeavors to design a game in which the behavior of strategic players results in the socially desired outcome.

Chapter VI

CONCLUSION

Peer-to-Peer (P2P) systems have emerged as an important paradigm for distributed storage in that they aim at efficiently exploiting untapped storage resources available in a wide base of peers. Data are outsourced to several heterogonous storage sites in the network, the major expected outcome being an increased data availability and reliability, while also achieving reduced storage maintenance costs, and high scalability. Addressing security issues in such P2P storage applications represents an indispensable part of the solution satisfying these requirements. Security relies on low level cryptographic primitives, remote data possession verification protocols, for observing malicious and selfish behaviors. Such an assessment of peer behavior is crucial to the more complex enforcement of cooperation, which is necessary due to the self-organized nature of P2P networks. It is also crucial to address open issues, such as how to mitigate denial of service attempts to the long-term storage as well as to the security and storage maintenance functions.

REFERENCES

[1] Akamai technologies, inc. http://www.akamai.com/
[2] Alfred J. Menezes, Paul C. van Oorschot, and Scott A. Vanstone. Handbook of Applied Cryptography. CRC Press, 1996.
[3] AllMyData Tahoe. http://allmydata.org/
[4] Amazon. http://www.amazon.com/
[5] Andrew C. Huang, Benjamin C. Ling, Shankar Ponnekanti, and Armando Fox. Pervasive computing: What is it good for?. In Proceedings of the ACM International Workshop on Data Engineering for Wireless and Mobile Access, pages 84-91, Seattle, WA, August 1999. ACM Press.
[6] Anind K. Dey and Gregory D. Abowd. CybreMinder: A context-aware system for supporting reminders. In Proceedings of Second International Symposium on Handheld and Ubiquitous Computing, HUC 2000, pages 172-186, Bristol, UK, September 2000. Springer Verlag.
[7] Antony Rowstron and Peter Druschel. Pastry: Scalable, distributed object location and routing for large-scale peer-to-peer systems. In Proceeding of the IFIP/ACMInternational Conference on Distributed Systems Platforms, Heidelberg, Germany, November 2001.
[8] Ari Juels and Burton S. Kaliski PORs: Proofs of retrievability for large files. Cryptology ePrint archive, June 2007. Report 2007/243.
[9] Attila Weyland, Thomas Staub and Torsten Braun. Comparison of Incentive-based Cooperation Strategies for Hybrid Networks. 3rd International Conference on Wired/Wireless Internet Communications (WWIC 2005), pp 169-180, ISBN: 3-540-25899-X, Xanthi, Greece, May 11-13, 2005.
[10] Audun Jøsang and Roslan Ismail. The Beta Reputation System. In Proceedings of the 15th, Bled Electronic Commerce Conference, Bled, Slovenia, June 2002.

[11] Audun Jøsang, Roslan Ismail, and Colin Boyd. A Survey of Trust and Reputation Systems for Online Service Provision. In Proceedings of Decision Support Systems, 2005.
[12] Ben Y. Zhao, John Kubiatowicz, and Anthony D. Joseph. Tapestry: An infrastructure for fault-tolerant wide-area location and routing. Technical Report UCB//CSD-01-1141, University of California, Berkeley, April 2000.
[13] BitTorrent. http://www.bittorrent.com/
[14] Bogdan C. Popescu, Bruno Crispo and Andrew S. Tanenbaum. Safe and Private Data Sharing with Turtle: Friends Team-Up and Beat the System. In 12th International Workshop on Security Protocols, Cambridge, UK, April 2004.
[15] Brian Neil Levine, Clay Shields, and N. Boris Margolin. A Survey of Solutions to the Sybil Attack. Technical Report 2006-052, University of Massachusetts Amherst, Amherst, MA, October 2006.
[16] Bridge Q. Zhao, John C. S. Lui, Dah-Ming Chiu. Analysis of Adaptive Protocols for P2P Networks. In IEEE INFOCOM 2009.
[17] Daniel Stutzbach and Reza Rejaie. Towards a Better Understanding of Churn in Peer-to-Peer Networks. Technical Report CIS-TR-04-06, University of Oregon, November 2004.
[18] David Goldschlag, Michael Reed, and Paul Syverson. Onion Routing for Anonymous and Private Internet Connections. Communications of the ACM, vol. 42, num. 2, February 1999.
[19] Décio Luiz Gazzoni Filho and Paulo Sérgio Licciardi Messeder Barreto. Demonstrating data possession and uncheatable data transfer. In IACR Cryptology ePrint Archive, 2006.
[20] Douglas Samuel Jones and B. D. Sleeman. Differential Equations and Mathematical Biology. London: Allen & Unwin, 1983.
[21] eBay. http://ebay.com
[22] Ee-Chien Chang and Jia Xu. Remote Integrity Check with Dishonest Storage Server. ESORICS 2008: 223-237.
[23] Emil Sit and Robert Morris. Security Considerations for P2P Distributed Hash Tables. IPTPS 2002.
[24] Emmanuelle Anceaume and Aina Ravoaja. Incentive-Based Robust Reputation Mechanism for P2P Services. Research Report PI 1816 (2006), IRISA, http://hal.inria.fr/inria-00121609/fr/
[25] Francesc Sebe, Josep Domingo-Ferrer, Antoni Martínez-Ballesté, Yves Deswarte, and Jean-Jacques Quisquater. Efficient Remote Data Possession Checking in Critical Information Infrastructures. IEEE

Transactions on Knowledge and Data Engineering, 06 Aug 2007. IEEE Computer Society Digital Library. IEEE Computer Society, 6 December 2007 http://doi.ieeecomputersociety.org/10.1109/TKDE.2007.190647

[26] François Lesueur, Ludovic Mé, and Valérie Viet Triem Tong. A Sybilproof Distributed Identity Management for P2P Networks In *Proceedings of the 13th IEEE Symposium on Computers and Communications (ISCC) 2008*, IEEE Computer Society, Marrakech, Morocco.

[27] François Lesueur, Ludovic Mé, Valérie Viet Triem Tong. Contrôle d'accès distribué à un réseau Pair-à-Pair. *SAR-SSI 2007*, Annecy, France.

[28] Frazer Bennett, Tristan Richardson, and Andy Harter. Teleporting - making applications mobile. In Proceedings of IEEE Workshop on Mobile Computing Systems and Applications, pages 82-84, Santa Cruz, California, December 1994. IEEE Computer Society Press.

[29] Garrett Hardin. The Tragedy of the Commons. Science, Vol. 162, No. 3859 (December 13, 1968), pp. 1243-1248.

[30] Gary E Bolton and Axel Ockenfels. ERC: a theory of equity, reciprocity, and competition. American Economic Review 90(1): 166-193, 2000.

[31] Gayatri Swamynathan, Ben Y. Zhao, Kevin C. Almeroth, S. Rao Jammalamadaka. Towards Reliable Reputations for Dynamic Networked Systems. In IEEE Proceedings on Symposium on Reliable Distributed Systems (SRDS'08), October 2008.

[32] Germano Caronni and Marcel Waldvogel. Establishing Trust in Distributed Storage Providers. In *Proceeding of the Third IEEE P2P Conference*, Linkoping 03, 2003.

[33] Giuseppe Ateniese and Randal Burns and Reza Curtmola and Joseph Herring and Lea Kissner and Zachary Peterson and Dawn Song. Provable data possession at untrusted stores. In *Proceedings of the 14th ACM conference on Computer and communications security*, ACM, 2007, 598-609.

[34] Gnutella. http://www.gnutella.com/
[35] Google. http://www.google.com/
[36] Grokster. http://www.grokster.com/
[37] Haifeng Yu, Michael Kaminsky, Phillip B. Gibbons, and Abraham Flaxman. SybilGuard: defending against sybil attacks via social networks. SIGCOMM 2006: 267-278.

[38] Hannelore Brandt and Karl Sigmund. The good, the bad and the discriminator--errors in direct and indirect reciprocity. Journal of

Theoretical Biology, Volume 239, Issue 2, 21 March 2006, Pages 183-194.
[39] Hovav Shacham and Brent Waters. Compact Proofs of Retrievability. ASIACRYPT 2008: 90-107.
[40] iMesh. http://imesh.com
[41] Ion Stoica, Robert Morris, David Karger, M. Frans Kaashoek and Hari Balakrishnan. Chord: A scalable peer-to-peer lookup service for internet applications. In Proceedings of SIGCOMM, San Diego, CA, Aug. 27–31, 2001.
[42] Jian Liang, Rakesh Kumar, and Keith W. Ross. The FastTrack overlay: A measurement study. Computer Networks, 50, 842-858, 2006.
[43] Jinyang Li and Frank Dabek. F2F: reliable storage in open networks. In Proceedings of the 5th International Workshop on Peer-to-Peer Systems (IPTPS), February 2006.
[44] John Kubiatowicz, Davic Bindel, Yan Chen, Steven Czerwinski, Patrick Eaton, Dennis Geels, Ramakrishna Gummadi, Sean Rhea, Hakim Weatherspoon, Westley Weimer, Chris Wells, Ben Zhao. OceanStore: An architecture for global-scale persistent storage. In *Proceedings of the Ninth international Conference on Architectural Support for Programming Languages and Operating Systems* (ASPLOS 2000), Nov. 2000.
[45] John R. Douceur. The Sybil attack. In Proceedings of the 1st International Workshop on Peer-to-Peer Systems (IPTPS'02). MIT Faculty Club, Cambridge, MA, 2002.
[46] KaZaA. http://www.kazaa.com/
[47] Kenji Koyama, Ueli Maurer, Tatsuaki Okamoto, and Scott Vanstone. New Public-Key Schemes Based on Elliptic Curves over the Ring Zn. Advances in Cryptology - CRYPTO '91, Lecture Notes in Computer Science, Springer-Verlag, vol. 576, pp. 252-266, Aug 1991.
[48] Kevin Lai, Michal Feldman, Ion Stoica, and John Chuang. Incentives for Cooperation in Peer-to-Peer Networks. In Proceedings of the 1st Workshop on Economics of Peer-to-Peer Systems, UC Berkeley, Berkeley, California, USA, June 2003.
[49] Landon P. Cox and Brian D. Noble. Pastiche: making backup cheap and easy. in Proceedings of the Fifth USENIX Symposium on Operating Systems Design and Implementation, Boston, MA, December 2002.
[50] Larry Page, Sergey Brin, R. Motwani, and T. Winograd. The PageRank Citation Ranking: Bringing Order to the Web. Technical report, Stanford Digital Library Technologies Project, 1998.

[51] Laszlo Toka and Patrick Maillé. Managing a peer-to-peer backup system: does imposed fairness socially outperform a revenue-driven monopoly?. 4th International Workshop on Grid Economics and Business Models (GECON 2007), August 28, 2007, Rennes, France, pp 150-163.

[52] Levente Buttyan and Jean-Pierre Hubaux. Stimulating Cooperation in Self-Organizing Mobile Ad Hoc Networks. ACM/Kluwer Mobile Networks and Applications, 8(5), October 2003.

[53] Lik Mui, Mojdeh Mohtashemi, Cheewee Ang, Peter Szolovits, and Ari Halberstadt. Ratings in Distributed Systems: A Bayesian Approach. In Proceedings of the Workshop on Information Technologies and Systems (WITS), 2001.

[54] Manuel Blum, William S. Evans, Peter Gemmell, Sampath Kannan, and Moni Naor. Checking the Correctness of Memories. Algorithmica 12(2/3): 225-244 (1994).

[55] Mark Lillibridge, Sameh Elnikety, Andrew Birrell, Mike Burrows, and Michael Isard. A Cooperative Internet Backup Scheme. In *Proceedings of the 2003 Usenix Annual Technical Conference* (General Track), pp. 29-41, San Antonio, Texas, June 2003.

[56] Markus Jakobsson, Jean-Pierre Hubaux, and Levente Buttyan. A Micro-Payment Scheme Encouraging Collaboration in Multi-Hop Cellular Networks. In Proceedings of Financial Crypto, La Guadeloupe, Jan. 2003.

[57] Michael Beigl. MemoClip: A location-based remembrance appliance. Personal Technologies, 4(4):230-233, September 2000.

[58] Michael Piatek, Tomas Isdal, Thomas Anderson, and Arvind Krishnamurthy. Do incentives build robustness in BitTorrent?. In Proceedings of the ACM/USENIX Fourth Symposium on Networked Systems Design and Implementation (NSDI 2007), 2007.

[59] Michal Feldman and John Chuang. The Evolution of Cooperation under Cheap Pseudonyms. CEC 2005: 284-291.

[60] Michal Feldman, Christos Papadimitriou, John Chuang and Ion Stoica. Free-Riding and Whitewashing in Peer-to-Peer Systems. Selected Areas in Communications, IEEE Journal on, Vol. 24, No. 5. (2006), pp. 1010-1019.

[61] Michal Feldman, Kevin Lai, Ion Stoica, and John Chuang. Robust Incentive Techniques for Peer-to-Peer Networks. Proceedings of ACM E-Commerce Conference (EC'04), May 2004.

[62] Miguel Castro, Peter Druschel, Ayalvadi Ganesh, Antony Rowstron and Dan S. Wallach. Secure routing for structured peer-to-peer overlay networks. *Symposium on Operating Systems and Implementation, OSDI'02*, Boston, MA, December 2002.
[63] Mihir Bellare, Oded Goldreich and Shafi Goldwasser. Incremental Cryptography and Application to Virus Protection. STOC 1995: 45-56.
[64] Ming Zhong, Kai Shen, Joel I. Seiferas. The Convergence-Guaranteed Random Walk and Its Applications in Peer-to-Peer Networks. IEEE Trans. Computers 57(5): 619-633 (2008).
[65] Moni Naor and Guy N. Rothblum. The Complexity of Online Memory Checking. FOCS 2005: 573-584.
[66] Morpheus. http://www.morpheus.com/
[67] Mudhakar Srivatsa and Ling Liu. Countering Targeted File Attacks using LocationGuard. In Proceedings of the 14th USENIX Security Symposium, to appear August 2005.
[68] N. Asokan, Matthias Schunter, and Michael Waidner. Optimistic Protocols for Fair Exchange. In Proceedings of the 4th ACM Conference on Computer and Communications Security, Zurich, April 1997.
[69] N. Asokan, Victor Shoup, and Michael Waidner. Asynchronous protocols for optimistic fair exchange. In Proceeding of the IEEE Symposium on Security and Privacy, 1998, 3-6 May, p. 86-99, Oakland, CA, USA.
[70] Napster. http://www.napster.com/
[71] Natalia Marmasse and Chris Schmandt. Location-aware information delivery with ComMotion. In Proceedings of Second International Symposium on Handheld and Ubiquitous Computing, HUC 2000, pages 157-171, Bristol, UK, September 2000. Springer Verlag.
[72] Neal Koblitz. Elliptic curve cryptosystems. Mathematics of Computation, 48 (1987), 203-209.
[73] Nouha Oualha and Yves Roudier. A Game Theoretical Approach in Securing P2P Storage against Whitewashers. In the 5th International Workshop on Collaborative Peer-to-Peer Systems (COPS'09), June 29 - July 1, 2009, Groningen, Netherlands.
[74] Nouha Oualha and Yves Roudier. Evolutionary game for peer-to-peer storage audits. In the 3rd International Workshop on Self-Organizing Systems (IWSOS'08), December 10-12, Vienna, Austria.
[75] Nouha Oualha and Yves Roudier. Reputation and Audits for Self-Organizing Storage. In the 1st Workshop on Security in Opportunistic

and SOCial Networks (SOSOC 2008), Istanbul, Turkey, September 2008.
[76] Nouha Oualha and Yves Roudier. Reputation and Audits for Self-Organizing Storage. In the 1st Workshop on Security in Opportunistic and SOCial Networks (SOSOC 2008), Istanbul, Turkey, September 2008.
[77] Nouha Oualha and Yves Roudier. Securing ad hoc storage through probabilistic cooperation assessment. 3rd Workshop on Cryptography for Ad hoc Networks, July 8th, 2007, Wroclaw, Poland. Electronic Notes in theoretical computer science, Volume 192, N°2, May 26, 2008, pp 17-29.
[78] Nouha Oualha, Melek Önen, and Yves Roudier. A Security Protocol for Self-Organizing Data Storage. 23rd International Information Security Conference (SEC 2008), Milan, Italy, September 2008.
[79] Nouha Oualha, Pietro Michiardi, and Yves Roudier. A game theoretic model of a protocol for data possession verification. TSPUC 2007, IEEE International Workshop on Trust, Security, and Privacy for Ubiquitous Computing, June 18, 2007, Helsinki, Finland.
[80] Patrick P. C. Lee, John C. S. Lui and David K. Y. Yau. Distributed collaborative key agreement and authentication protocols for dynamic peer group. IEEE/ACM Transactions on Networking, 2006.
[81] Peter Druschel and Antony Rowstron. PAST: A large-scale, persistent peer-to-peer storage utility. In *Proceedings of HotOS VIII*, May 2001.
[82] Philipp Obreiter and Jens Nimis. A Taxonomy of Incentive Patterns - the Design Space of Incentives for Cooperation. Technical Report, Universität Karlsruhe, Faculty of Informatics, 2003.
[83] Philippe Golle, Kevin Leyton-Brown, Ilya Mironov. Incentives for Sharing in Peer-to-Peer Networks. In Proceedings of the 3rd ACM conference on Electronic Commerce, October 2001.
[84] Philippe Golle, Stanislaw Jarecki, Ilya Mironov. Cryptographic Primitives Enforcing Communication and Storage Complexity. In *Proceeding of Financial Crypto 2002*.
[85] Pietro Michiardi. Cooperation enforcement and network security mechanisms for mobile ad hoc networks. PhD Thesis, December 14th, 2004.
[86] Roger R. Dingledine. The Free Haven project: Design and deployment of an anonymous secure data haven. Master's thesis, MIT, June 2000.
[87] Sepandar D. Kamvar, Mario T. Schlosser, and Hector Garcia-Molina. The EigenTrust Algorithm for Reputation Management in P2P

Networks. In Proceedings of the Twelfth International World Wide Web Conference, Budapest, May 2003.
[88] Shane Balfe, Amit D. Lakhani and Kenneth G. Paterson. Trusted Computing: Providing security for Peer-to-Peer Networks. In Proceedings of the 5th International Conference on Peer-to-Peer Computing (P2P), 2005.
[89] Sylvia Ratnasamy, Paul Francis, Mark Handley, Richard Karp, and Scott Shenker. A scalable content-addressable network. In Proceedings of SIGCOMM, San Diego, CA, Aug. 27–31, 2001.
[90] Thai-Lai Pham, Georg Schneider, and Stuart Goose. Exploiting location-based composite devices to support and facilitate situated ubiquitous computing. In Proceedings of Second International Symposium on Handheld and Ubiquitous Computing, HUC 2000, pages 143-156, Bristol, UK, September 2000. Springer Verlag.
[91] Theodore L. Turocy and Bernhard von Stengel. Game theory. Cdam Research report lse-cdam-2001-09, London School of Economics, October 2001.
[92] Thomas Schwarz, and Ethan L. Miller. Store, forget, and check: Using algebraic signatures to check remotely administered storage. In *Proceedings of the IEEE Int'l Conference on Distributed Computing Systems* (ICDCS '06), July 2006.
[93] UbiStorage. http://www.ubistorage.com/
[94] Victor Miller. Uses of elliptic curves in cryptography Advances in Cryptology, Proceedings of Crypto'85, Lecture Notes in Computer Science, 218 (1986), Springer-Verlag, 417-426.
[95] Vivek Vishnumurthy, Sangeeth Chandrakumar and Emin Gun Sirer. KARMA: A Secure Economic Framework for P2P Resource Sharing. In *Proceedings of the Workshop on the Economics of Peer-to-Peer Systems*, Berkeley, California, June 2003.
[96] Wenrui Zhao, Yang Chen, Mostafa Ammar, Mark Corner, Brian Levine, and Ellen Zegura. Capacity Enhancement using Throwboxes in DTNs. IEEE International Conference on Mobile Ad hoc and Sensor Systems (MASS), Vancouver, Canada, October 2006.
[97] Wuala. http://wua.la/en/home.html
[98] Yves Deswarte, Jean-Jacques Quisquater, and Ayda Saïdane. Remote Integrity Checking. In *Proceedings of Sixth Working Conference on Integrity and Internal Control in Information Systems* (IICIS), 2004.

INDEX

A

ACM, 51, 52, 53, 55, 56, 57
ad hoc network, x, 1, 39, 57
adaptation, 5
administrative, 9
agent, 46
agents, 46
air, 33
algorithm, 19, 31
alternative, 2, 29, 39, 47
alternatives, 46
altruism, 46
application, ix, x, 1, 2, 3, 4, 10, 13, 15, 27, 31, 34
applied mathematics, 37
argon, 29
assessment, xi, xii, 7, 10, 30, 49, 57
assignment, 44
asymmetry, 42
attacker, 15, 31
attacks, 3, 4, 14, 15, 31, 32, 44, 53
auditing, xii, 37
authentication, 4, 19, 57
authority, xii, 3, 4, 8, 29, 33, 34, 44
availability, ix, 3, 5, 9, 20, 45

B

back, xi, 13, 15, 44
bandwidth, 32, 46
banking, 34
banks, 32
barter, xii, 11, 29
behavior, ix, xi, xii, 2, 3, 7, 9, 10, 11, 13, 16, 30, 35, 37, 39, 42, 43, 44, 45, 48, 49
beliefs, 48
benefits, xii, 29, 46
blocks, 17, 18
bootstrap, 4

C

cache, x, 1
CEC, 55
censorship, 3
certification, 4, 31, 32
cheating, 3
CIS, 52
classification, xi, 8
codes, xi, 13
coding, 5
collaboration, 55
collusion, ix, 31
commerce, 33
commons, 3
communication, 17, 19, 21, 27, 31
communication overhead, 19, 27, 31
compensation, 35, 47
competition, 53
complexity, 5, 17, 19, 21, 25, 27
computation, 20, 21, 25, 27
computer science, 57

computing, x, 1, 15, 20, 51, 58
confidence, x, 7
confidentiality, ix, 3
connectivity, 5
conservation, 5, 16
construction, xi, 13, 16, 18, 19, 22
consumption, 41
context-aware, 2, 51
control, xii, 4, 5, 29
convergence, 43, 45
COPS, 56
correlation, 10
corruption, ix, 15, 16, 17
cost-effective, ix, 2
costs, x, xii, 1, 5, 14, 20, 32, 49
CPU, 14, 21, 22
CRC, 51
cryptographic, xii, 3, 6, 18, 34, 45, 49
cryptography, 21, 22, 23, 58
currency, 34
cycles, x, 1

D

data availability, x, xi, xii, 1, 9, 13, 49
data structure, 16
data transfer, 52
Decision Support Systems, 52
decisions, 37, 38
decoding, 16
defects, 29
definition, 48
delivery, 2, 56
denial, xii, 49
destruction, ix, 15, 43
detection, 16, 30, 32, 48
diminishing returns, 45
direct observation, 30
directives, x
distribution, 4, 31, 33, 34, 45
donor, 43
donors, 43
download, 46
durability, 5, 8
duration, 5

dynamic environment, 20
dynamic systems, 31

E

encoding, 16
encryption, 3, 25, 26
energy, 2
environment, 4, 32
equilibrium, 38, 39, 43, 45, 46, 48
equity, 53
evolution, xii, 37, 41, 43
evolutionary games, x
exposure, 30

F

failure, 2, 4, 8, 20, 21, 44
fairness, 32, 34, 42, 55
fault tolerance, 20
fee, 45
feedback, 9, 10
fees, 4
fingerprints, 17
fitness, 43
flooding, 15, 30
flow, 32
free-ride, xii, 30, 37, 45, 46
friendship, 8, 32

G

game theory, 29, 38, 48
games, x, xii, 37, 38, 39, 40
generation, 2, 42
goals, 3
google, 53
government, vi
GPD, 42
graph, 31
groups, 5
growth, 1, 43
growth rate, 43

H

hardness, 21, 23, 26
heterogeneity, 44
heterogeneous, 48
hybrid, 18

I

identification, 4
identity, 3
implementation, 32, 33
incentive, x, xii, 5, 6, 9, 10, 27, 29, 37, 39, 40, 41, 42, 43, 44
incentives, x, xi, xii, 8, 9, 10, 11, 27, 29, 30, 37, 39, 42, 44, 46, 55
indices, 16, 17
inequality, 31
infinite, 38
information sharing, 8
information system, 58
information technology, 1
infrastructure, xi, xii, 2, 13, 31, 32, 33, 37, 52
innovation, 1
integrity, xi, 3, 10, 13, 18, 19
interaction, 3, 35, 39
interactions, x, 7, 8, 9, 11, 33, 37, 38, 46
internet, 54
invasive, 16
investment, 32
iteration, 48

J

joining, xi, 7

L

language, 37
large-scale, x, 34, 51, 57
learning, 41
lifetime, 30

limitation, 16
location, 2, 51, 52, 55, 58
losses, 34
lower prices, 35

M

magnetic, vi
maintenance, x, xii, 1, 49
malicious, ix, xii, 27, 49
management, 2, 5
mapping, 2
5atrix, 40
measurement, 54
membership, 4, 45
memory, x, 16, 17, 18, 21
messages, 2, 5, 10, 14, 15, 27
mirror, 41
MIT, 54, 57
mobility, 2
modeling, 39, 48
models, xi, 7, 37, 39, 41
modules, 33
modulus, 17, 19
money, 4, 35
monopoly, 48, 55
multiplication, 23, 26, 27

N

nash equilibrium, 38, 39, 40, 48
nodes, 2, 33, 39, 40
normalization, 42

O

onion, 4
online, 33, 34, 45
operating system, 33
operator, 48
overlay, 8, 54, 56

P

packet forwarding, x, 1, 10
packets, 2, 39
parameter, 25, 27, 31, 41, 43, 44
PDP, 17, 22
peer, ix, x, xi, xii, 1, 3, 4, 5, 7, 9, 10, 11, 13, 15, 17, 19, 26, 27, 29, 30, 31, 32, 33, 34, 35, 37, 39, 40, 41, 42, 43, 45, 46, 47, 49, 51, 54, 55, 56, 57
peer assessment, 10
peer group, 57
peers, ix, x, xi, xii, 2, 3, 4, 7, 8, 9, 10, 11, 13, 20, 21, 27, 29, 30, 31, 32, 33, 34, 35, 37, 39, 40, 41, 42, 43, 44, 45, 46, 49
penalties, 4
penalty, 11, 30, 32, 44, 45, 46
periodic, 5, 6, 13, 20
personal computers, x, 1
perturbations, 41
platforms, 33
play, 33, 38, 43
Poland, 57
poor, 38
population, 4, 31, 39, 40, 43, 48
population size, 43
power, 3
preference, 38
prices, 47, 48
primitives, ix, xi, xii, 13, 15, 21, 23, 49
privacy, ix
private, 43
probability, 16, 17, 26, 40, 41, 42, 44, 45, 46
profit, 15
property, vi, 5, 26, 39
protection, xi, 13
protocol, 14, 15, 17, 19, 21, 23, 24, 25, 26, 27, 30, 33, 34, 35, 48, 57
protocols, x, xi, xii, 1, 7, 10, 13, 16, 21, 27, 31, 34, 37, 49, 56, 57
public, 9, 16, 19, 21
punishment, xii, 29, 44, 48

Q

quality of service, 2
query, 17
quotas, 34

R

random, 15, 16, 17, 18, 19, 20, 25, 32
random numbers, 17, 20, 25
rationality, 3
reception, 25
reciprocity, 11, 30, 53
recovery, 16, 17, 18, 22
redundancy, ix, 5
regular, 5
relationships, xi, 7, 8, 9, 10, 32
reliability, ix, xii, 5, 9, 31, 49
replication, 2, 4, 5, 8, 15, 43, 44, 45
reputation, xi, xii, 7, 9, 10, 11, 29, 30, 31, 32, 39, 42, 43
resource management, 5
resources, ix, x, xii, 1, 9, 10, 11, 32, 34, 42, 44, 48, 49
revenue, 55
rewards, 47
risk, 15
robustness, 30, 41, 55
routing, x, 1, 4, 31, 51, 52, 56

S

SAR, 53
scalability, x, xii, 1, 4, 20, 23, 33, 49
scalable, 2, 32, 34, 54, 58
search, 18, 33
secret, 16, 17, 18, 19, 20, 21, 25, 26
secrets, 8
security, ix, xii, 6, 14, 15, 19, 23, 25, 27, 43, 49, 53, 57, 58
seed, 16, 20, 25
self, x, xi, 1, 13, 20, 55, 56, 57
self-interest, xii, 29
self-organization, x, 1, 2, 33

self-organizing, xi, 13, 23, 29, 39
sensitivity, 41
services, vi, x, 1, 2, 31, 42, 46
sharing, ix, x, 1, 3, 4, 5, 8, 30, 33, 34, 46, 47
short-term, 11
simulation, 44, 45, 46, 47
sites, x, xii, 1, 8, 49
social dilemma, x, 3
social network, 53
social relations, 8
social relationships, 8
social welfare, 4, 45, 48
SSI, 53
stability, 9, 42
starvation, 35
storage, ix, x, xi, xii, 1, 2, 3, 4, 5, 8, 9, 10, 13, 14, 15, 19, 20, 21, 25, 26, 27, 30, 32, 33, 34, 35, 37, 43, 44, 45, 48, 49, 54, 56, 57, 58
strategies, xii, 10, 37, 38, 39, 40, 41, 43, 46
supply, 34, 47
switching, 42
symbols, 16, 18
symmetry, 47
synchronization, 34

T

taxonomy, 7, 8
telephony, x, 1
tension, 3
third party, 4, 33, 34
threats, 2
threshold, 34

tolerance, x, 1, 20
tracking, 33
trade, xi, 7, 20
trading, 30, 32
transactions, 31, 34, 42
transfer, 46, 52
transformation, 21, 22
trees, 18
trust, x, xi, 7, 8, 9, 10, 11, 32
turnover, 42, 45, 46

U

UCB, 52
uncertainty, 48
updating, 34
upload, 30, 46
user data, ix, 16

V

validation, x, 22
values, 16, 17, 31, 34, 38, 43
variables, 46
vector, 41
VoIP, ix
vulnerability, 31

W

welfare, x, 3, 45
wireless, 2